You're Smarter Than They Make You Feel

You're Smarter Than They Make You Feel

How the Experts Intimidate Us
and What We Can Do About It

PAULA J. CAPLAN

THE FREE PRESS
A Division of Macmillan, Inc.
NEW YORK

Maxwell Macmillan Canada
TORONTO

Maxwell Macmillan International
NEW YORK   OXFORD   SINGAPORE   SYDNEY

The Free Press
A Division of Macmillan, Inc.
866 Third Avenue, New York, N.Y. 10022

Maxwell Macmillan Canada, Inc.
1200 Eglinton Avenue East
Suite 200
Don Mills, Ontario M3C 3N1

Macmillan, Inc. is part of the Maxwell Communication Group of Companies.

Printed in the United States of America

printing number

1 2 3 4 5 6 7 8 9 10

Library of Congress Cataloging-in-Publication Data

Caplan, Paula J.
  You're smarter than they make you feel: how the experts
intimidate us and what we can do about it/Paula J. Caplan.
      p. cm.
  Includes bibliographical references and index.
    ISBN 0–02–905235–1
  1. Consumer education.   2. Psychology, Applied.   I. Title.
TX335.C333   1994
640'.73—dc20

93–39291
CIP

For

Susan Gilbert Carrell, Gina Feldberg, Maureen Gans,
Nikki Gerrard, June Larkin, Donna Sharon,
and Rachel Josefowitz Siegel—

Who have strengthened and empowered with
great love and humor

Contents

Acknowledgments

This book was born in the years I was growing up in Springfield, Missouri, because of the values, the principles, and the love in which I was immersed there, thanks to my parents, Tac Karchmer Caplan and Jerry Caplan; my grandparents, Esther Milner Karchmer and Nathan Karchmer; and my uncle, Billy Karchmer. There is no way to express adequately my gratitude and love for them for all of that. Not only have they set wonderful examples but they have also made me feel constantly supported, respected, and loved.

My heartfelt thanks also go to my mother, the first person I told about my idea for this book, for the enthusiasm and encouragement she showed me at that time—and all the other times. I also want to thank my editor, Susan Arellano, for her warmth, her enthusiasm, her wonderful ideas, and her generosity of spirit that make our meetings occasions of great interest and delight for me; my son, Jeremy Benjamin Caplan, and Sally Armstrong, Gina Feldberg, and Phyllis Poore Woollen for their encouragement early in the process of planning and writing; Susan Gilbert Carrell, Nikki Gerrard, Bob Lescher, Carol Tavris, and Jeremy for their feedback on the book proposal; Margaret Grant for her kindness and thoughtful comments; Graham Berman, Diane Goudie, and June Larkin for their perceptive and detailed suggestions on the entire manuscript and for the great gift of their time; my daughter, Emily Julia Caplan, for creating the title and for putting up with me as I wrote; my father, my mother, Winston Davis, Donna

Sharon, Pat Turner, and David Turner for their helpful comments, and Edward Cone for his superb copyediting. With regard to this book, as with all of my work, I am grateful to my father for being constantly watchful for relevant, useful articles and ideas—he provides loving and thoughtful research assistance that makes me eagerly anticipate opening the envelopes he sends.

. . . none but the most conscionable human beings ever question the true nature of the institutions that are theoretically protecting them.

—Tom Robbins

For an unjust system to work for any prolonged period of time, it is necessary that the masses of people believe they deserve the injustice.

—Monica Sjoo and Barbara Mor

. . . all growth is the discovery of power—or powers.

—Paul Horgan

1

You're Smarter Than They Make You Feel

When we feel worse instead of better after seeking help, most of us blame ourselves. Our achievement-oriented, education-obsessed society promotes this attitude: We assume we are lacking in intelligence, education, or resourcefulness. "I probably didn't ask the right questions or make my case well enough," we think. Or "I should have pushed harder—or not as hard." My primary aim in this book is to urge consumers to ask questions, especially the question, "Is it really all my fault that I didn't get the help that I sought, or is something else happening?"

We go into a system seeking help, and we may or may not get that help; but *whether or not we do*, our experiences in that system may make us feel powerless and stupid. This book is not about how to "beat the system" or get what you need from authorities and institutions, but it is about how to avoid letting the system beat you and beat you down. Whether or not a system ultimately serves you, you shouldn't have to feel worse about yourself after having been through it.

1

Unjustified self-blame not only paralyzes us but actually carries us down unproductive trails, because the failure to get the most appropriate help is usually not the consumer's fault. My research on hundreds of therapists who do child custody assessments, for instance, showed that much of their work is biased, subjective, and frankly uninformed.[1] In these emotionally explosive assessments—which lead to recommendations to judges about where children of divorce should live—many of the assessors rarely even try to obtain information from anyone except the disputing parents, and some never even see the children who are the subjects of the dispute. Many admit that they do not carry out their *legal* responsibility for reporting to child welfare authorities when one parent alleges that the other has physically or sexually abused the children; and even when child welfare workers are investigating such allegations, many tell the court which parent they believe should have custody *before* the child welfare workers have determined whether or not abuse occurred. Despite such biases, the divorced parents who are these assessors' clients usually feel that whatever goes wrong proves their own failings, and they may spend countless hours trying to figure out what *they* can do better, rather than realizing that the professionals' judgment may be poor. After all, the assessors are supposedly well-trained social workers, psychologists, and psychiatrists who are experts on human behavior!

And consider what happened to my friend Ellen. Unexpectedly and abruptly, she lost her job. Worried about how to support her children, she immediately made an appointment at the unemployment office. She hoped to start drawing unemployment payments as soon as possible while looking diligently for a job in the depths of the recession. As Ellen faced the unemployment interviewer across his huge desk, she recalled that, when her sister had applied for unemployment benefits, her interviewer had become angry as she described her situation and had yelled, "You be quiet and wait for *me* to ask the questions!" Determined to handle her interview properly, Ellen said "Hello" and then waited for her interviewer to speak. When he asked questions, she limited her answers strictly to his inquiries. She was puzzled by his clearly increasing irritation and at last asked timidly, "Shall I just tell you the whole story of how I lost my job?" He exploded, "Of course, damn it! That's why you're here!" Ellen found it hard to keep from bursting into tears, and she felt ashamed, as though she had done something terribly wrong. Not until she told a friend about her experience did she realize that she was not at fault. She had been in a no-win situation.

We are told we are lucky to live in the age of information, and we are told that knowledge is power. But most of us feel stupid and powerless when we come smack up against experts from the medical, mental health, governmental, legal, or educational fields or other authorities whom we *expect* to inform, help, and empower us. As children, we believe we'll feel more powerful and effective as we grow up, but the truth is often the reverse: The older we get, expecting to feel truly powerful, knowledgeable, and in control at last, the more we feel helpless, inadequate, and ineffective. And those feelings are usually the same, regardless of the institution, system, or expert with which we are dealing. The proliferation of support groups and self-help books for what seems like every imaginable problem and situation is a reflection of how helpless and isolated people feel. So is our culture's epidemic of low self-esteem, which has us rushing misguidedly into therapy, wondering if our "toxic parents" or "dysfunctional families" are to blame. Although therapy can be helpful when the problems really do come from our close relationships, too often we waste time and energy looking mistakenly within ourselves or our families for the sources of our feelings of impotence and shame, when it could be more to the point to look to the authorities, systems, and experts in our society.

We need to know how and why institutions and experts so often make us feel stupid and powerless and how to surmount the stupefying effects of such encounters. This book is addressed to those issues. It is especially important to understand how this happens, because not only do they make us feel bad about ourselves but they can also do profound, sweeping, or permanent harm to us or to those we love.

How I have wished, in writing down the stories of frustration and disempowerment that follow, that I could have told you in each case, "If only the consumer or client had done X or had not done Y, all would have been well." Other writers have certainly offered advice on how to beat various systems. But I was impelled to write this book because so often nothing works—the agency director refuses our requests, or the psychiatric association dismisses our legitimate complaint against one of their members, or we can't get an investigative reporter to broadcast the story of injustice done to a family member, or we choose not to file lawsuits or initiate human rights or sexual or racial harassment proceedings because we know what it is likely to cost us in time, money, energy, and freedom to enjoy other aspects of our lives. And when we can do nothing more, or when we deem it necessary to stop trying to obtain the services we or our loved ones need, *we absolutely must not waste more time and energy unjustifiably blaming and berating ourselves*.

Virtually every adult has felt inadequate and helpless when dealing with authorities and experts who seem to have the information we need or the power to help us. We've all had some maddening experience such as listening hard but not understanding when a doctor or lawyer tells us about our medical or legal situation, when a psychologist or teacher interprets our child's test results, or when a person we've hired to repair our home or car doesn't quite fully explain why we supposedly need expensive work done. Even if we don't feel foolish asking them to explain better, we may feel helpless, because we don't know where or how to begin asking questions.

We feel flooded these days with information, mystified by technology, and lost in bureaucratic mazes. Most of us feel there's so much we don't understand, so much we cannot grasp. What is certainly true is that if we don't understand what happens to us, we cannot hope to recognize that it is not our fault.

I have seen wealthy, white, highly educated men—children of the 1960s who long ago learned *in principle* that "authorities" don't always aim to help—weep from feeling defeated and impotent when they *as individuals* had to deal with powerful systems or so-called "experts." I have watched them try desperately to figure out which of their own failings did them in. For most people, it's easier to see that others are mistreated by systems and authorities *through no fault of their own* than it is to stop finding fault with themselves. Strangely enough, blaming ourselves can give us a feeling of hope; after all, we feel, if we are to blame, then perhaps if we just try harder or eradicate our faults, we may get the help or support we need.[2] And if we keep trying and do not succeed, we may become so depressed that we decide we need therapy. As a therapist for many years, I saw that much of people's pain came from their low self-esteem and shame as a result of these kinds of experiences.

An intelligent, well-educated woman, after reading one of my books, wrote to tell me, "I am still very much traumatized by what a male doctor did to my body with a knife even though I protested and begged him not to and now I carry the guilt of, 'I should have been able to stop him.'" Indeed, in a culture in which we have to turn so often to experts and authorities for help, a lot of people spend much of the time feeling powerless and inadequate. In a recent discussion group, the often-maligned women's magazines were named by women as great reading material precisely because their articles do not make women readers feel stupid—an all-too-rare experience for many women.

Even those who, in the eyes of others, seem powerful are not exempt from such feelings, and many accomplished, well-known individuals have recounted how various systems and authorities have made them feel inadequate, stupid, hopeless, or powerless. It is worth looking at a few of these.

Long after graduating from a highly respected women's college, feminist journalist Gloria Steinem realized that as students, she and her classmates had been encouraged to devalue women, what she called female students "getting an A-plus in self-denigration."[3] She described the ways this devaluation was promoted through the selection of reading assignments, the kinds of theories they were taught, and the scarcity of women in positions of power and respect within academia.

For Maya Angelou, the talented poet who read one of her poems at President Clinton's inauguration, one of the most disempowering and demoralizing experiences was hearing a speech by the white male politician who addressed her grammar school graduation. In *I Know Why the Caged Bird Sings*, Angelou writes, the politician first announced the wonderful things that had been done for the *white* school in town, including bringing in a well-known artist to teach art and providing the newest microscopes and chemistry equipment for their laboratory. Then he said if they reelected him, he would have the playing field paved at the Black students' school and he praised a football player who had graduated from that school. Having initially been almost unbearably excited about her graduation ceremony, Angelou felt this way after hearing the speech:

> The white kids were going to have a chance to become Galileos and Madame Curies and Edisons and Gaugins, and our boys (the girls weren't even in on it) would try to be Jesse Owenses and Joe Louises. . . .
>
> Graduation, the hush-hush magic time of frills and gifts and congratulations and diplomas, was finished for me before my name was called. The meticulous maps, drawn in three colors of ink, learning and spelling decasyllabic words, memorizing the whole of *The Rape of Lucrece*—it was for nothing. [The speaker] had exposed us.
>
> We were maids and farmers, handymen and washerwomen, and anything higher that we aspired to was farcical and presumptuous.[4]

Jeffrey Moussaieff Masson, a brilliant Sanskrit professor with a Ph.D. from Harvard who later became curator of the Sigmund Freud Archives, describes in his fascinating book, *Final analysis: The making and unmaking of a psychoanalyst*, the psychological abuse to which he was subjected by his analyst, Irvine Schiffer.[5] Masson cites instances of Schiffer's yelling at him, lying to him outright, taking telephone calls and chatting about cars and "portfolios" while Masson lay on the couch during his sessions, and "explaining" Masson's problems by claiming, for instance, that his wife was ugly. Finally, Masson reports, Schiffer tried to insist that Masson make him a co-author on a paper that Masson and Masson's wife had written, although Schiffer had done no work on it whatsoever.

Many people have asked Masson why he, an intelligent, well-educated white male, continued for years to pay Schiffer and to believe that Schiffer had something to offer him. Masson's reasons are ones to which most of us can relate: When we need help, the wish to believe in someone is powerful. Masson had to avoid upsetting his psychoanalyst because he needed Schiffer's help in three ways. First, he wanted to become an analyst himself and, in order to do so, had to complete analysis as a patient with one of the few "training analysts," and Schiffer was one. And, of course, any negative comments from Schiffer to the psychoanalysts' organization could have meant professional death for Masson. Second, after spending years in academia, Masson had become disillusioned by the pretentiousness and the politics he saw there, and he came to psychoanalysis hoping and believing that here, at last, were people who cared above all about the truth and were honest and trustworthy. If he couldn't believe in them, he wasn't sure whether there was anyone left whom he could respect. Third, on his own, Masson had been unable to overcome some major personal problems, and he believed that, as a training analyst, whatever Schiffer was doing in their work together must be aimed at "curing" him. And when Masson did question him, Schiffer usually let Masson know that he would never surmount his psychological problems unless he believed that Schiffer knew best. Sometimes, Masson writes, Schiffer didn't even bother making that claim but simply threatened to destroy Masson's chances of becoming analyst if he didn't do as Schiffer instructed.

The appalling mistreatment of both the late Pulitzer prize–winning poet Anne Sexton and the immensely creative writer and sculptor Kate Millett by the psychiatric system has been documented in great and horrifying detail,[6] and the stories of others who have been failed or subjected to various kinds of abuse by other professionals and systems that are supposed to help consumers are legion.

Those of you who, like me, have been in positions of authority in at least one such system probably know that that experience by no means keeps us from feeling baffled and impotent when we need help or information from another system. Some of us are even more flabbergasted when we become consumers in the system in which we work. Physician Oliver Sacks describes his own experience of this in his book about becoming a patient in the neurology system in which he had been employed.[7] And those of us who have been in positions of authority know that, although some of us care little about the clients/consumers, many do care but either are unaware of our effects on help seekers or feel unable to do better. This issue is treated at length in Chapter 4, but throughout the book it is important to keep in mind that not all clients/consumers are good or easy to serve and not all people in authority are bad or malicious.

THE GOOD NEWS

The good news is that *we don't have to feel this way*. And the best way to begin to feel better is by understanding the *techniques* used for making us feel stupid and powerless. Over the past twenty-five years, as I have worked and observed in many different fields, I have been struck by how astonishingly similar are the most common techniques that various institutions, authorities, and experts use for keeping their consumers in the dark and disempowering them. That is why I decided to write this book. But it's interesting that we all, at least occasionally in our daily lives, use the kinds of distancing techniques the authorities use. As a result, when you read about the techniques authorities use to disempower us, they will probably strike you as familiar. You may have used them yourself, or friends and family members may have used them with you.

Later in this chapter, I address the question "Why do we blame ourselves?" and then the issue of why individuals react somewhat differently to mystifying and frustrating systems. In Chapters 2 and 3, I describe the most common disempowering techniques. Throughout this book, when I use terms like *institutions, systems,* or *authorities,* most of what I will be saying applies to a whole spectrum of people who have power over us—from plumbers and automobile mechanics to some weight-loss technique promoters to representatives of the legal, medical, mental health, governmental, and educational systems to individual salespeople in stores who do not want to help when we return defective goods. Clearly, some of these people have far more powerful effects on our lives than others, because it is fairly easy to switch grocery stores or plumbers and more difficult to change lawyers or doctors or therapists; but we may have *no* other options if such institutions as the court, unemployment, or certain other governmental systems fail us. In Chapter 4, I discuss *why* the authorities and the so-called experts too often act in hurtful, or at least unhelpful, ways, and in Chapters 5, 6, and 7, I name the major obstacles that keep authorities from thinking critically about how they deal with consumers and those that keep consumers from thinking critically about, and questioning, authorities. In Chapter 8, I describe some ways people have used to avoid feeling stupid and powerless when they are badly treated. As I have said, I do not promise to tell you how to beat the system, transform institutions, or make any authority into a true helper. But I can tell you that having handy a concise, numbered list of the hurtful techniques will *help* you feel better and keep a clear view of reality. And some of these strategies *may* even increase your chances of getting the help you need.

I intend this book to be used as a kind of handbook. Instead of agonizing over what you should have asked the doctor about the treatment of your mother's illness or what you did to make the bank manager refuse your request for a loan, I hope your first thought will be to flip to pages 23–25, glance at the techniques list, and realize, "That person was using Technique Number 14 on me. Now I understand why I felt so inept." And then I hope you will turn to pages 155–178 and ask yourself which suggestions from the "What You Can Do" list strike you as helpful to you.

I am a clinical, research, and community psychologist and have had intensive experience—as consumer/client/patient, as expert, or as both—in many of the institutions that do this kind of harm. I have worked as a clinical psychologist; a researcher; the second-in-command of a hospital-based children's learning

clinic; a government agency employee; an assessor and therapist in a family court clinic; a consultant on a host of parenting,
divorce and custody, juvenile delinquency, child welfare,
weight-loss, and other issues; and an expert witness and adviser to the courts for a wide range of cases and to a provincial
ethical and disciplinary body for psychologists and one for
lawyers. I have also trained other people to do these kinds of
work. I have worked as a community psychologist, primarily
specializing in the empowerment of previously relatively powerless individuals and groups. Over many years, I have also
been a client of several lawyers and therapists, a student in
schools and universities, a patient of physicians and in hospitals, an applicant for help from a government agency, and a
complainant to professional discipline bodies about the conduct of a few of their members.

I know firsthand both how frustrated and powerless clients
can feel and how many of the authorities' and experts' *unnecessary* practices and pretenses cause those feelings. I have
learned a great deal about what makes patients, clients, and
consumers in a wide variety of arenas feel that they are too stupid to understand what the experts in these "helping professions" and other services are telling them. I have also learned
firsthand, and from talking with others who have been in positions of authority, that some of those who frustrate and hurt
clients and consumers in these ways would be terribly upset if
they knew they were doing this, whereas others don't much
care how they affect others (more about this in Chapter 4).

We easily forget that *feeling* stupid does not mean *being* stupid. And the more we know about the techniques that most
commonly make us feel bad about ourselves, the more quickly
they'll spring to mind when they are being used on us, and the
less likely we'll be to blame ourselves. As a consumer, I have
many times gone from feeling stupid and ashamed to understanding that I was not to blame. The key to these changes has
usually been information or support from other people. For
instance, when I bought a computer, I had an awful time learning to use it, although I read the manual with great care. After
spending one particularly terrible night trying until 3:00 A.M. to

get the machine to do what the manual assured me it would do, I feared I was developing computer-induced psychosis. Fortunately, my eleven-year-old son knew a great deal about computers and, after listening to my tale of woe, told me that many manuals are appallingly badly written, and crucial steps are often omitted. He went over my manual with me and pointed out where this applied in my case.

We can spend hours reading up on learning disabilities when our children are having academic problems or on contract law if we are headed for small-claims court, and that information may be very helpful; but knowing enormous amounts of technical information about a field is no guarantee that we will be aware of the damaging ways the particular system uses that information selectively, conceals information, interprets it in distorted or unpredictable ways, or otherwise hurts the people it is supposed to serve. And although knowing the details of a carburetor's inner workings tells us nothing about psychiatrists' ways of deciding whom to label as mentally ill, identifying the ways that some automobile mechanics make us feel stupid and powerless will probably help us notice similar techniques more readily when a psychiatrist uses them. In addition, if we know the common patterns of disempowerment and misuses of knowledge ahead of time, we won't feel so daunted if we need to learn a lot of technical information in a particular field. Because I want the focus of this book to be clearly on the disempowering techniques and how to deal with them, I reluctantly decided not to attempt to review or list the large number of books aimed at educating consumers about a whole range of systems and services, such as the workings of automobiles, the law of contracts, natural remedies for illnesses, and the structures and operations of government agencies and corporations.

I am continually amazed by how many educated people are not aware of how various systems disempower them and make them feel stupid—or if they do understand, they understand only in principle and often don't recognize it when it happens to them. They make general statements like "I know The System is cold, impersonal, and mystifying," but when a *particular* system has a devastating impact on them, they don't know what hit them. Or they may be familiar with medical and hospital workings, for instance, but do not realize how many of the same principles apply to the legal system. I knew a man who was highly informed about many aspects of the business world but was helpless in the face of the legal and psychotherapy systems in his divorce and child custody suit.

WHY DO WE FEEL THIS WAY?

When there's trouble, why are so many of us so quick to assume that the fault is our own? After all, it would be easier and we'd feel a lot better if we blamed it on the institution in question—or even on "evil forces" or a strange conjunction of the stars. Many factors—both social and psychological—contribute to this self-blame tendency.

Our trouble begins with the myth that authorities and experts are there to help us. Some want to provide help and indeed do so effectively, but the *myth* is that they're *all* eager and able to do so. Such systems as the medical, legal, and unemployment ones were indeed established to serve their clients and do so for many; but systems grow unwieldy and bureaucratic and take on lives of their own. Over time, then, some of their workers' energy goes into maintaining the system, its power, and its status rather than into serving clients. This book is about how that directly affects the consumer, because the myth that systems and experts are there to help makes it hard to pull back and see that sometimes they do us more harm than good. As a result, when something goes wrong, that myth makes us look inward for the source of the trouble.

Most major institutions and experts are protected from questions about their intentions, functioning, and shortcomings by the high regard in which they are held in our society. Even though many citizens may complain about the complexity and problems in, for instance, the healthcare system, when a real live physician enters the room, their responses are likely to range from quietly respectful through somewhat intimidated to frankly awestruck. Our feeling that, as individuals, we cannot possibly hold major systems and experts accountable is fed by our knowledge that they are backed by high-powered law firms whom they pay to defend them from such confrontations. Many people—including, I confess, me—first learned from the film *Class Action* that some automobile manufacturers decide whether or not to recall potentially dangerous cars for purely financial reasons. In that movie, a manufacturer knows that a certain percentage of its cars will explode under certain circumstances. However, the executives calculate that they can save money by *not* recalling the cars, keeping their information to themselves, and eventually paying off the injured (or those whose relatives are killed) who bother to file complaints. This turns out to be a widespread practice even under less dramatic circumstances. For instance, now that insidious health problems that come from working in some airtight buildings constructed during the energy crisis are becoming known, some owners of these buildings are choosing to do nothing proactive. They prefer to pay off those few sufferers who (1) make the connection between the building's condition and their symptoms and (2) decide to take the risks involved in filing a complaint or a lawsuit. Indeed, it does cost less money to pay off a few such people than to do the expensive work of cleaning up such buildings.

Another reason we blame ourselves for feeling stupid and powerless when confronting a massive system is that we don't have enough knowledge about the system to be able to point out where it is at fault. As novelist A. S. Byatt has written, "The unknown is hard to get at, because it is unknown."[8] A huge impediment to our understanding most systems is the truly astonishing proliferation of jargon in this century. Yet the people within most fields ardently resist getting rid of their jargon. I had helped run a clinic for children with learning problems, had co-authored a book for a major publishing company on the subject, and had taught for years in a school psychology program aimed at training psychologists to identify and treat such problems, but I remained perplexed every time I heard such claims as "This child has an auditory processing deficit." Over the years, I learned that if I asked five different learning disability teachers and psychologists to explain what that meant that the child could not do, I got five different answers—and many of those were filled with more unclear jargon. At last, I wrote an essay about how riddled that field is with mystifying and imprecise language and with lack of consensus about what learning-disabled children can and cannot do. But every major learning disabilities journal turned it down before it was accepted by a fine but far less traditional periodical.[9]

Another factor that makes us tend to blame ourselves is our culture's intense preoccupation with achievements, the worship of self-sufficiency, and the concept of "toughing it out" alone. The nineteenth-century individualist tradition has led us to assume that, if we just try hard enough, we can do anything. Therefore, by implication, if we do not achieve what we want, it must be because we are lazy, stupid, or inept. As I have written, the powerful groups in any society keep their power partly by finding scapegoats whom they can blame when anything goes wrong.[10] In this way, they preserve the fiction that the institutions where the power resides are incorruptible and blameless. Sometimes individuals are, in effect, scapegoated one at a time, as when each ill or injured person struggles through the maze of applying to a government agency for workers' compensation. When that is combined with whole new languages of jargon and complex systems of operation that have developed over recent decades, we often see no option *but* self-blame and feelings of humiliation after being stymied by an unfamiliar system.

A major psychological factor that leads us to blame ourselves rather than institutions is the need to believe we are in control, as mentioned earlier. From those who have written about abused women and children, and from the research on concentration camp inmates, hostages, and people who have been brainwashed, we have learned that horribly mistreated people often cling to their sanity by trying to keep *some* control—or the belief that they have some control—over *something*. When we know we are likely to be subjected to infuriating or horrible treatment, sometimes the best we can manage is to convince ourselves that we *could* prevent it from happening if only we could find the right technique, the magic words, the way to appease the frustrator or the tormentor. First thing Monday morning, the plumber told Mary he'd be right there to fix her overflowing toilet, so she phoned her workplace to say she wouldn't be in until after lunch. After waiting three hours for the plumber to show up, she began to wonder whether she had misunderstood what he had told her, whether, if she called him now and said as clearly as possible that her situation was urgent, he would come over immediately. Wondering about this gave her the feeling that she might have some control.

We are all the more likely to try to figure out where *we* have failed if we can't escape from the situation or would risk death or harm if we tried to escape. So, for instance, suppose you have been injured in a car accident and need a financial settlement in order to support your children. If your lawyer, Mr. Jones, seems to be ignoring your instructions or mishandling your case, you may consider changing lawyers. You learn, though, that that would mean paying the new lawyer a lot of money for reading through the thick files your current lawyer has amassed, as well as paying the new one for meeting with you and hearing you tell the whole, painful story yet again. You may also worry, justifiably, that the new lawyer will suspect you of being a troublemaker for having fired your previous one. In view of this, you decide to stick with Mr. Jones, but what do you do about his unsatisfactory performance? Even if you consider something as mild as speaking to him politely about his failure to return your calls or his commission of crucial errors, you know that you cannot afford to alienate a lawyer who may ultimately represent you in court. Your only way to hold on to some semblance of sanity may be to spend your time searching for "just the right way" to express your concerns or trying to understand how you have "failed" to make your instructions crystal-clear to Mr. Jones. Soul searching and introspection can feel much less risky than taking action in the real world. Fortunately, in some situations more promising options are available. But in those with no such options, it is essential to avoid adding to the pain of that limitation the shame and anguish of holding yourself to blame.

In his book *The great divide: Second thoughts on the Ameri-*

can dream, Studs Terkel illustrates this immersion in self-blame in the face of unresponsive systems. In his example, the unresponsive system is a recession-burdened economic system including banks and a government that failed to provide adequate support for small farmers.[11] According to Terkel, Lou Anne Kling, state coordinator for the Minnesota Department of Agriculture's farm advocate program, told the story of a young man who lives with his parents on their farm:

> He comes home and tells dad, "I bought a new tractor today."
> The dad says, "You shouldn't have done it. We can't afford it."
> The son says, "You old duffer, you don't know what you're talkin'
> about. My God, So-and-So bought one."
>
> The kid gets mad and huffs outside. And dad sits in a chair
> and says, "If I'd have been a better farmer, we'd have had more
> money and would have been able to buy that new tractor. I'm
> gonna cash in my life insurance policy and pay that bill so my
> son don't know that we're in tough shape." He'll hide it from his
> son as long as he can and let him continue to think it's okay. The
> majority of farmers still feel that they're failures. They didn't
> produce right, they didn't farm right. They've been farming forty
> years and they don't think they've done anything right. They
> blame themselves.[12]

As this story illustrates, during a recession, institutions tend to become less helpful and more punitive, when more people genuinely need help. And then individuals already feeling lousy because of losing their jobs are made to feel even worse when they confront the banks, unemployment offices, and so on.

To summarize, the reasons we blame ourselves when systems and experts fail to serve us include the following:

1. The myth that they are always there to help
2. The dilemma that we may not know enough about the system to know where or how it could be at fault
3. Our society's stress on the individual's achievement and self-sufficiency
4. Our need to believe that we have some control
5. Our having so much at stake that it feels risky to blame the system

Underlying most of these reasons are the powerful forces in our culture that suppress questioning or critical thinking about authorities, which is the subject of Chapters 5, 6, and 7. This suppression is key, because if we do not question a system that fails us, whom *can* we blame but ourselves?

IT HITS EACH ONE OF US DIFFERENTLY

It is unpleasant and upsetting to be frustrated or mistreated by a major institution, but some of the forms that upset takes vary, depending on precisely who we are. If you are *used* to being active and effective, a real problem solver in most spheres of your life, you may find it easier to cope because your analytical, problem-solving abilities will come in handy, but what will be harder will be the unfamiliarity of feeling impotent. If, however, you feel that most aspects of your life are beyond your control, a new incident can drive you still deeper into despair.

The extent to which, in the family where you grew up, individuals' efforts were believed to be *the* key to success will also probably make a difference. In your early life if you were not encouraged to make allowances for individuals treated badly by more powerful people and groups—for instance, because of their race, sexual orientation, or age—then you may find it hard to make such allowances for yourself. And in your early experiences, the more you felt valued and appreciated for yourself—by family members, teachers, friends, and so on—the more likely you are to be able to recognize when your frustration or defeat by a system is not your fault.

Your sex may also shape your reaction to feeling disempowered and stupid. The traditional female role includes helplessness in the face of powerful people and systems, and many women have chronically low self-esteem, so women may not feel very surprised to feel stupid and powerless—but that does not mean that still another experience of such feelings is not devastating.[13] By contrast, the traditional male role includes wielding power and being intelligent as crucial elements, so men disempowered by a major institution may feel not only frustration as human beings but also shame and fear about deviating from the demands of masculinity. In other words, for women, the most likely reaction may be, "So, this is just one more time I turn out to be inadequate—how depressing, but no surprise," while for men it may be, "A real man is *never* inadequate! I am in control at work and at home! This is terrifying and unfamiliar!" Or for many men it might be, "A real man is never inadequate. It's humiliating enough that I feel inadequate at work, and now this, too!"

A large body of research shows that both women and men tend to attribute women's failures to their own, unavoidable inadequacies, whereas they attribute men's failures to chance factors or the unfairness of the system.[14] In keeping with this, when a heterosexual couple is jointly disempowered by a system, they may both turn on the woman for being unable to fight it better. As we have seen after such "acts of God" as Hurricane Andrew, in the face of feelings of powerlessness and inadequacy men's violence against women often increases—a significant and serious danger. Indeed, the social pressure on men always to feel powerful and in control causes some men to panic—and become violent—when they feel powerless.

Frequently, heterosexual couples decide that the man should take the major role in trying to hold the system accountable, because they recognize that men often get more respect than women. This decision underlines further the woman's lack of power but also puts still more pressure on the man to deliver positive results. An example from my own experience comes to mind. I phoned the men who replaced my wooden front steps to inform them that the first rain after they completed their work collected in a pool in each new stair. They told me that was "normal." But when one of my male friends confronted them, they clearly assumed that, being a man, he knew the facts about construction. They acknowledged that they had installed the steps the wrong way, and they immediately corrected their mistake. I was glad to have the job done properly, but I was frustrated by having been treated with such disdain and dishonesty. My male friend was glad to help me but irritated by having to take time out to deal with the situation.

What can mitigate the negative effects for people of either

sex is that some of us know from working in institutions our-selves that they can operate in hurtful, uncaring, even crazy-making ways, and therefore the surprise element will be missing. But some people, as noted, find it hard to apply what they already know about the coldness or corruption of a famil-iar system to one that is currently defeating them.

Everything that applies to sex differences in these situations also applies to differences of race, class, age, and physical and mental condition. People who are not white, at least middle class, neither too old nor too young, and not able-bodied and apparently of at least average intelligence or conventionally attractive and emotionally well adjusted are more likely to have experiences similar to those described above for women. Liv-ing daily as a target for sexism, racism, classism, ageism, ableism, and weightism reduces the chances that you will have the emotional and physical resources to do anything other than blame yourself, become depressed, and give up when you are mistreated by a system. The one bright spot in this picture is that people aware of being oppressed for the above reasons are often quicker than others to recognize that further mistreat-ment is not their fault but rather the result of the way the sys-tem operates.[15]

If you are a baby boomer, a child of the 1960s, questioning authorities may feel relatively comfortable, so once you focus your attention on the commonality of techniques used by the various systems, you may be well on your way to avoiding feel-ings of stupidity and impotence. However, you have also very likely been raised to believe that you are better educated—or simply know more—than your parents; if that is the case, you are at risk for feeling even more humiliated (and blaming your-self) when you fail to get what you need from, or win a battle against, a major institution.

WHERE DO WE GO FROM HERE?

To live fully and gloriously in the world, we need to feel emboldened to try new things. But the more system-based frus-tration we encounter, the more we experience the problem of snowballing meekness—the rock of Sisyphus feels larger and heavier, and we feel smaller and weaker, less able to venture into the world, to become fully engaged in living. When that happens, the sensible thing *seems* to be to stop trying, and then the space taken up by the arenas we hesitate to enter becomes increasingly larger, like the widening circles made by a pebble tossed in a pool. But once we can easily spot the common techniques used to disempower and stupefy us, we can waste less energy and time on misguided self-blame (and use our energy more constructively) and thereby minimize unnecessary damage to our self-esteem. Then, too, we are better prepared to choose from among our alternatives—deciding whether or not to continue to try to get what little blood might ultimately come from a stony system or whether to direct our energies elsewhere. If we decide to continue to operate within—or against—an institution, having the knowledge of its common disempowering techniques at our fingertips is like knowing how high the hedge is before we begin our jump. At least as we return to interact with that system, we can use our resources with greater wisdom and a clearer sense of what is likely to work. We are in a better position to sharpen our skills, gather support, keep notes, document everything from the beginning, or do whatever else might help us achieve our aims. At the very least, we can make another try with less risk of feeling terrible about ourselves if we don't triumph this time. That kind of knowledge can afford us certain kinds of power and certain kinds of control.

This matters a great deal, not only for the sake of our individual growth, empowerment, and self-esteem but also for all those who may look to us as role models or as sources of ideas about how to cope in an apparently overwhelming world.

Insofar as this is a self-help book, an important word of warning is in order. Sometimes the readers of self-help books try the recommended steps and, if they do not work, assume they failed because they didn't do the tasks carefully or skillfully enough. If you read this book and still find that you cannot beat the system or even that your self-esteem doesn't fully recover, remember that what may feel like your individual fail-ure is probably actually further evidence of the power of the system you are up against. After all, anyone raised during the twentieth century is so accustomed to dealing with disempow-ering systems as hardly to notice how they work. It would be unrealistic to expect that reading a book like this once could counteract a lifetime of interpreting institutions' lack of posi-tive, helpful responses to you as proof that you do not deserve such responses. The tenacity of patterns of self-blaming and institution-excusing can be broken only if you take such con-crete steps as referring to the techniques list as often and for as many months or years as necessary, and acting on some of the straightforward suggestions for "What You Can Do." You will be your own best judge of which steps you need most to repeat or expand.

And now, we are about to plunge into the heart of the matter: Identifying some of the most frequently used techniques that characterize our major institutions' damaging and demeaning treatment of us. Chapter 2 is about techniques that involve pri-marily what authorities do and do not say, and Chapter 3 is about the frustrating things that they do or fail to do—although there is a great deal of overlap between verbal and other kinds of techniques. The subject of Chapter 4 is what motivates authorities and experts to act as they do, and Chapters 5, 6, and 7 are about why so few consumers question what authori-ties say and do, why so few authorities think critically about their own work and that of other authorities, and why so many unthinkingly accept what they are told. When you are a con-sumer, you'll be more resilient in dealing with experts and authorities if you understand what motivates them when they treat you badly, and you'll be better fortified if you also are aware of some of the factors that tend to inhibit both their and your inclination to ask questions about how the system works. Chapters 4 through 7 are important, but I've placed them after Chapters 2 and 3 because, if you are currently grappling with a frustrating system or expert, you are likely to find Chapters 2 and 3 (and Chapter 8) more immediately useful, and you may want to turn directly to them. Chapter 8 is about ways to avoid feeling stupid and powerless—and even, sometimes, to get the information or the help you need—in these kinds of situations.

In the examples I have given so far, I have mentioned mental health professionals, government unemployment office workers, doctors, auto mechanics and manufacturers, lawyers, teachers, office building owners, learning disability specialists, bankers, and home construction workers. It may seem bizarre to write in a single book about the techniques used by such a variety of authorities and about the kinds of motives that impel them, but it is useful to do so. We live in increasingly service-based economies, in which as private citizens or through taxes we pay for a vast variety of services, and any time we need service or expert advice, that puts us in a vulnerable, one-down position: the potential provider of service or crucial advice has power over us because of our need. And as I've said, people with power tend to use similar techniques in dealing with the less powerful.[16] It makes sense to deal with such an array of fields in one book because they share a great many basic techniques and motives.

You will notice, however, that I include more medical and psychotherapy examples than others. There are several reasons for that, because I could have drawn from a great number of fields and quoted from the many fine books that reveal the inner workings of various institutions and agencies. First of all, when our body or our psychological state is at stake, we are in many ways at our most vulnerable, and so when medical and mental health systems fail us, the consequences can be devastating, even life-threatening. In some ways, these professionals have the greatest power over us, because although some lucky people may go through life without having to deal much or at all with lawyers, unemployment interviewers, or bank managers, few of us these days escape contact with physicians and therapists, and often that contact is under intense, upsetting circumstances. Although most of us have had some maddening experiences with other professionals or with people who repair various pipes, wires, appliances, or structures in our homes, the devastation we typically experience when dealing with them tends not to be as great as when dealing with doctors or therapists who fail to serve us or our loved ones well. Second, people are most likely to have had contact with these systems, so they are the most familiar. Third, these are the ones in which I have had the most direct experience, so I have many of their stories to tell. Finally, the sum of money we pay to doctors is enormous, and healthcare costs are the number one cause of bankruptcy in the United States. This makes it all the more poignant and unforgivable when the professionals in that system provide poor services. It may seem to you that I am singling out physicians and therapists for criticism, so I want to state clearly that I know some terrific physicians and terrific therapists. But that doesn't mean that we can count on them all to be good.

A word of warning is in order: In reading about how people have been hurt by the techniques described in Chapters 2 and 3, you may feel the relief of connection because you've had similar experiences. Or you may start to feel overwhelmed by all of the frustration and harm that these people endured. If you feel the latter, remember that the point of those stories is not to depress you but rather to illustrate the techniques so that you can recognize which ones have been hurtful to you. Remember, too, that Chapter 8 is composed entirely of information about strategies people have found useful for recovering from some of the ill effects of those techniques and for avoiding being hit hard by them the next time they are encountered.

In the next two chapters, before I describe the techniques, I include a quick look at what they are.

THE DISEMPOWERING TECHNIQUES: A QUICK PREVIEW

Here is just a brief summary of some of the techniques most commonly used to disempower us and make us feel stupid. They are discussed in detail in Chapters 2 and 3, but this quick guide is provided in the hope that even a rapid scan of it may speed you on the way to relief from the way you are feeling now and help you decide which parts of the following chapters may be the most relevant for you. Often, just having a label for the way you are mistreated feels good, because it helps you stop feeling that the fault is all your own. In addition, simply having such a list may in some cases help you get the assistance you need by enabling you to point out succinctly to the authorities what they are doing. Those who haven't realized what they are doing but want to serve you may be more likely to do so when you describe clearly what they are doing that is not addressed to your needs.

As you read through examples of these techniques in the next two chapters, you may find yourself identifying so much with the consumers that you will start to feel as though all experts are intentionally, maliciously difficult. For two reasons it is useful to remember that, although some people use these techniques knowingly or at least without concern for their impact on consumers, some people in some systems do help us some of the time, and some people who unintentionally do not help would regret it if they realized it. It is important to keep this in mind because it is realistic, and recalling it may help keep you from despairing about ever getting what you need from any system.

What They Say and What They Don't Say

1. They use jargon and mystifying technical language.
2. They divide and conquer.
3. They give you some, but not all, of the information you need—and don't tell you that that's not all there is to know.
4. They make the simple seem complex and incomprehensible.
5. They present *ideas* and *opinions* as though they were indisputable *truths*.
6. They do not tell you all your options.
7. They tell you to leave it to them, because they are the experts.
8. They call it what it isn't.
9. They claim that what you want them to do is not their responsibility.
10. They blame you for what is not your fault.

What They Do and What They Don't Do

11. They fragment you as a person.
12. They use outright fakery (either intentionally or not).
13. They transform what you say into "proof" that you are bad, crazy, or wrong.
14. They are unwilling to listen to you.
15. They simply do not answer your questions, or they may outright refuse to answer them.
16. They intimidate you.
17. They do a little but pretend they have done a lot.
18. They behave irresponsibly, immorally, or even viciously.
19. They support other people in their system instead of helping you.
20. They change the rules as they wish but pretend rules are absolute and unchangeable.

2

What They Say and What They Don't Say

One reason self-help and consciousness-raising groups have been so effective is that we feel lighter and less alienated when we see how similar our experiences have been to those of other people. When I was a teenager, I read somewhere that most teenagers suffer a great deal from the feeling that their emotions and thoughts are bizarre and peculiar to them. That rang so true for me, and it led me to try, in tiny steps at first, telling other people what I felt and thought and asking them if any of that fit with their experiences. As long as I choose reasonably humane people, rarely does anyone look at me as though I were crazy and tell me they have never heard of such a thing. Often, hearing me label what I have felt or how I have been treated has been a great relief to others, because they have heard me describing their own experience—and vice versa. Few things are as depressing as feeling that the negative aspects of our lives are unique to us. So, although many of the examples in this chapter and the next are about terrible situations, the familiarity of some of the situations and your feeling of connection to some of the consumers in them should be encouraging.

I tell the following stories because most of us are much quicker to blame ourselves than to blame others when they are in similar situations. I hope that it will be easier for you to see first how other people's disempowerment and feelings of inadequacy or stupidity were undeserved, and that then you will be able to transfer that perspective to your own situation.

In these two chapters, most of the examples come from cases I know about directly, but the principles apply to many institutions and experts across the board. Even if the institutions or experts that have frustrated and disempowered you are not specifically mentioned here, you will probably recognize the techniques themselves as those that have been used to make you feel terrible. Most of the examples come from situations in which the consequences of the disempowering techniques are not only frustration and feelings of helplessness but also dangers to your health, your emotional well-being, your pocketbook, or your children or other loved ones. However, because people with some degree of power or authority in such an enormous range of settings use such similar techniques, I also include some less serious or even somewhat amusing ones.

As you read through the illustrations of the techniques in this chapter and the next, you may wonder *why* the authorities and experts behaved in that way and why the systems operate like that. As noted, in Chapter 4 I deal with some of the widely varying reasons for the authorities' behavior. However, for the client/consumer to feel better, it is not absolutely essential to comprehend how the systems are organized and operated in ways that hurt the people they are supposed to serve. To analyze the individual systems fully and is beyond the scope of this book, but I urge you to read some of the references in the bibliography if you want to explore these systems in more detail.

Because authorities and experts in so many realms use such similar techniques, I shall use the terms *authorities* and *experts* interchangeably, as well as the terms *consumers* and *clients*.

As you read the examples of the disempowering techniques and notice parallels between them and your own experiences, I urge you to jot down some notes about the specifics of your own situation, such as which techniques the frustrating authorities are using that cause you trouble. This may be helpful if you decide to return to the authorities, point out clearly and straight-forwardly which techniques they are using in your case, and see whether that might get you better service. Making notes will undoubtedly reduce your tendency to blame yourself for these frustrations, because seeing the specifics in black and white, under the categories of particular techniques, helps clarify where the problems really lie. According to Gloria Steinem, a project of the California Task-Force on Self-Esteem demonstrat-ed that simply writing down what made them feel either empow-ered or powerless had positive effects on students' feelings.[1]

And now we turn to the disempowering techniques them-selves.

1.   They use jargon and mystifying technical language.

In a recent Beetle Bailey cartoon, Sarge tells the doctor he doesn't feel well, and the doctor informs him, "You've got that thing that's going around." Sarge asks what he should do for it, and the doctor hands him some pills, saying, "Take some of this stuff." Sarge walks away, saying, "I like doctors who use med-ical terms you can understand."

A cardinal rule to remember is that *all jargon is in fact unnecessary* for talking to consumers, clients, and patients. Authorities and experts have absolutely no reason to use words that the average layperson cannot understand: "a century ago . . . the mathematician and astronomer Henri Poincaré . . . asked, 'Why is the reality most acceptable to science one that no small child can be expected to understand?' "[2]

When jargon is used, it usually makes fairly innocuous situa-tions seem worse than they really are and makes truly serious ones harder to deal with. In all cases, it makes the listener's job of understanding the message more difficult, and it certainly makes us feel that we are too stupid or uneducated to compre-hend what is happening to us or to those we love. In this way, importantly, it reduces the degree to which we feel in command of the information and in control of the situation. What first-year college student wouldn't be intimidated by a professor who lectures about "the need to deconstruct the hegemony of the discourse in this society that is dominated by an oligarchy"? And when someone's health is involved, jargon can be especially disconcerting, as in this example:

> When my son Jeremy was in grade school and we flew to Missouri to visit my parents one summer, Jeremy developed a bad rash on the backs of his knees. My father offered to take him to the dermatologist one afternoon and, when they returned, took me aside and reported with alarm and great solemnity, "The doctor said that Jeremy has a condition called 'atopic dermatitis,' and he needs to use this very special ointment on it several times a day." Because I had worked in a hospital and become familiar with some of the medical jargon, I was able to reassure my father by explaining that "atopic (or nonspecific) dermatitis" actually meant "skin irritation whose cause the dermatologist can't figure out" and that dermatologists prescribe the special ointment for a wide variety of rashes and irritations. I felt very angry that the doctor's use of technical language had caused my father so much unnecessary worry about his little grandson.

Even when the situation does not involve a health problem, an expert's use of jargon makes it harder for consumers to exercise any control over the service they are seeking:

> An air-conditioning salesman informs me that, when he receives complaints that the air conditioner his service people have installed is making a lot of noise, he tells the customer, "Your unit has hysteresis." If they persist in asking what that means, he replies, "That means vibrations of the laminations of the transformer." Naturally, they think they need to hire one of his service people to come back and repair the hysteresis, because what he doesn't tell them is that simply tapping the unit is a harmless and effective way to stop the noise without doing any harm.

Some jargon has absolutely devastating, long-term effects, as in the following example:

> Many therapists describe their unhappy patients as "masochists." The meaning of this term is a person who actually enjoys suffer-

ing or pain, something most people would regard as extremely strange and deeply disturbed. Most importantly, the term suggests that the source of the unhappiness is *within* the patient. One result of the use of this word is that the *real* causes of people's unhappiness—which are often outside of themselves, such as being treated in demeaning ways, underpaid, or abused—are often overlooked. I have talked with many people who were in therapy and learned from their therapists to think of themselves as "masochists." Usually, when they told their therapists that they truly did not enjoy suffering, their therapists replied, "Ah, not *consciously*, you don't. But *unconsciously*, you must—or else you wouldn't be unhappy!" As a consequence, many battered women have remained in relationships with the men who beat them, because their therapists had "taught" them that even if they left Fred, their sick unconscious drives would propel them inevitably toward yet another man who would abuse them. Through the use of such dangerous jargon, many people—most often women—have become more depressed after therapy, feeling even more hopeless about their ability to change their lives than before.[3] Even today, nearly a decade after I began work on this topic, I continue to hear contemporary stories like this.

When authorities baffle us with jargon, we can reduce its negative impact on us by thinking of its use as the Pig Latin Principle; that is, let us see jargon as a sophisticated and sophomoric form of children's use of Pig Latin or other made-up codes to make other children feel left out.

2. *They divide and conquer.*

Making you feel like you are the *only* person who has ever felt this way, filed such a complaint, or made such a request is a fast and easy way to make you feel isolated, weird, foolish, or even crazy. The implication is that everyone else in the world is different from you and can handle whatever it is you are objecting to. All other things being equal, this encourages you to fall silent.

> For my daughter Emily's tenth birthday party, I planned to make genuine Southern fried chicken for 12 children. The day before,

I bought four whole, cut-up fryers at a store whose advertising campaign focuses on the quality of their meat. When I opened package after package of the chicken to start cooking, vile odors drifted forth. Holding the chickens at arm's length while covering my mouth and nose with my other hand, I returned to the store and presented the reeking bag to the manager. I even told him that I had bought these for my daughter's birthday party, which was scheduled to begin two hours hence. There was no way he could have escaped the smell of those foul fowls, but he simply looked at me and said, "No one has ever before complained about our meat." I have to admit that I felt embarrassed when he first said that. The technique almost worked, because it deflected my attention from the problem at hand: four evil-smelling birds and a party about to begin. Had I not pictured my daughter's face, were I to return home empty-handed, I might have slunk away in silence. But I told him I suspected I was *not* the only person ever to complain, that it seemed to me beyond the realm of coincidence that all four chickens I had bought there the day before would just *happen* to be spoiled, and that frankly, I did not care whether I was the only person to complain, because the fact was that I quickly needed four fresh chickens. My request was granted.

A male farmer whom Studs Terkel interviewed described the use of the divide-and-conquer technique through the application of the label "radical" in a very serious situation:

Then I got involved with this farm group, and there is people just like me. They get tagged as radicals right away. 'Cause we're supposed to be civilized now. It's all right for some S.O.B. in a white shirt and tie to come along and take our farms away from us on paper. But it's not all right for us to try to keep him from doin' that. The minute we say we're not gonna let him do that, we become radicals.

. . . My banker even suggested, "You don't want to let your neighbors know that you're having financial trouble, 'cause you're the only one that's having trouble." I know several other farmers he's told that to. There's a neighbor down here two miles, we was meetin' each other on the road, we'd wave at each other but we wouldn't stop to talk to each other. He thought I was doin' all right and he was wonderin' how come, and I was wonderin' the same thing about him.[4]

3. *They give you some, but not all, of the information you need—and don't tell you that that's not all there is to know, or "A little learning is a dangerous thing."*

When we are dealing with professionals or with many government agencies, very often what we (or our tax dollars) are paying for is information. Although this book may help you get the information you need from those who are supposed to provide it, in some circumstances consumers cannot possibly know whether or not the information they have been given is complete. This happened to me in dealing with my insurance company last year:

> My dentist told me that much of the silver in my teeth needed to be replaced, and I was anxious to have the work completed as soon as possible. Before telling the dentist to begin, I telephoned my insurance company to see whether all of the replacements would be covered. The woman at the other end of the phone asked me, "What needs to be done?" and I replied, "Six fillings need to be replaced." She said, "Oh, that is all covered. No problem." I had the work done and submitted the proper forms to the insurance company. When the company sent a check for only a small portion of the cost, I phoned to ask for an explanation. I was informed that only part of the work was covered by my insurance plan, and when I protested that that was a different story than I had been given before, the woman explained, "When you originally called me, you said that you needed *fillings* replaced. But on the bill, I saw that some of them were inlays and some were outlays. You never told me that." I was flabbergasted. All my life, I had thought that the name for those silver things in the teeth was "fillings." Not being a dentist, I had never learned the technical distinctions among fillings, inlays, and outlays. And never before had I had occasion or need to learn them. I argued that the insurance woman ought not to assume that consumers know the technical language. I said, "When I said I needed fillings, I think you should have asked me

to check with the dentist to find out whether any were inlays or outlays." I also told her that I felt most consumers did not know these differences. I don't think that we consumers should be expected to be up on all of the details of every system with which we deal, but that means that, as in this case, we often think we have full information when in fact we do not.

When authorities conceal information or—either intentionally or unintentionally—give you *some* information but not all that you need, you are less likely to be able to achieve your goal, but you won't understand why you have failed. As in the fable of the blind men and the elephant, if you think you are trying to move a fan (the elephant's ear), you'll never figure out why it's so difficult unless you realize there's a whole huge beast attached to it.

What Johnston has written about physicians applies to a broad range of institutions and authorities:

> the medical profession disempowers its clients by withholding information and thus, coercing individuals into complying with physicians' directions. In the traditional form of health education, passive patients are provided with a minimum of information for the sole purpose of increasing patient compliance with professionals.[5]

Whether or not the doctor in the following example realized he hadn't given his patient full information, he went on record as saying he had told her everything. A journalist who was observing him chronicled this process:

> Patient 9: Smily ancient lady—all of 90. . . . He checks her pacemaker function, . . . Andersson says, "This particular model is doing fine. It's basically a three-year model now." Cryptic. She nods as if she understands. Leaves.
>
> He stops in his office. Dictates notes of the nine cases so far, very fast. Dictation on . . . lady with pacemaker includes this odd phrase: "Has been notified about possible malfunction of this model pacemaker."[6]

When not health but financial need is the issue, we may endure needless worry if those in authority provide us with only partial information:

If you think your bank manager believes that you told the truth on your financial application, you won't understand the reasons for the delay in approving your loan unless the manager—or someone else—has told you about the lengthy credit checks the bank requires.

Sometimes authorities' provision of only partial information has both legal and financial consequences, as in this story:

On a rainy day, Martin pulled his car over to the curb, got out, opened the door behind the driver's seat, and was lifting a parcel out of the back seat when the open door was hit by a car coming up from behind him. Sam, the other driver, immediately got out of his car and told Martin, "I wasn't really looking, and I know I was going too fast, and I didn't see your door until it was too late." Nevertheless, he took Martin to small-claims court, alleging that Martin's door should not have been opened and denying that he had been speeding and driving recklessly. He claimed that Martin's error had resulted in extensive damage to his car, far more than was actually the case. Martin suspected that Sam was trying to collect enough money to buy a new car. The day before the case was due to go to court, a man phoned Martin, said he was Sam's lawyer, and said that if Martin would pay 90 percent of the sum for which Sam was suing, they would settle the case out of court. Martin thought that was unreasonable, made a somewhat lower offer, and asked the lawyer to let him know Sam's response. He decided that he would settle out of court if it was a halfway reasonable sum. The lawyer did not call back. Martin had not hired a lawyer for himself, because he figured that the lawyer's fees would probably be more than what he would have to pay if he lost the case. The next day, what really galled Martin was not that the judge believed Sam's version over Martin's but what happened after the judge announced that he was deciding in Sam's favor. Sam's lawyer leapt to his feet and said, "Your Honor, yesterday we made an offer to settle this case out of court, and the defendant refused. Therefore, we ask that Your Honor order him to pay double my client's legal fees, in addition to the amount for damage to my client's car." The judge readily agreed to do so. Martin learned later that the small-claims court administrators are supposed to mail an information pamphlet to every plaintiff or defendant who is scheduled to go to their court. In the pamphlet, it is noted that if one party makes an offer to settle out of court and the other party refuses, then if the party who refuses is found guilty, they may be ordered to pay double the other's legal fees. The court administrators, it seemed, had simply neglected to send the pamphlet to Martin. When Martin wrote the court a letter objecting to this and asking to appeal the case based on that ground as well as others, the appeal was denied.

Authorities' purposeful concealment of relevant information has had appalling consequences. The infamous case of the U.S. military's withholding of information about victims of Agent Orange is one of the best-known examples, but there are many more. Pilisuk reports the following story of June Casey, who was a college sophomore in 1949. On a visit home in Washington state,

> her wavy brown hair fell out, never to grow again. She was diagnosed as a case of severe hypothyroidism. . . . her symptoms, particularly a chronic fatigue, never left her and made normal activities of life a source of strain. She endured one stillbirth and one miscarriage. . . . In 1986, June Casey came upon a 1950 report that had been withheld until then, which noted that a large escape of radiation had occurred at the Hanford Nuclear Weapons Facility at precisely the time that her symptoms began. . . . The report at last clarified the source of distress that the evasive answers of doctors and other officials had only intensified; it confirmed that the duress of her entire adult life was the result of decisions made by her own government. She was, in her own words, "a sacrificial lamb."[7]

People of both sexes have considered themselves hypochondriacal or even crazy because of the way they were treated when their doctors did not know how to explain their symptoms. Too often, doctors tell their patients, "There is no known cause for the pattern of symptoms you have described to me, so you must be imagining it, trying to get attention, or suffering some deep psychological disturbance." And then, especially when the patient is a woman, the doctor is likely to prescribe tranquilizers or sleeping pills. For men, who are expected to be physically strong and never get sick, it is especially unsettling to experience physical problems that they are told they must be imagining.

My father, Jerry Caplan, told me that someone once said, "You *cannot* beat me at *my* game or in my business," because you cannot know all the technical things that I know and that I won't let you know. In a nutshell, that is the reason that so much specialization and technology can be so dangerous—that if the experts don't choose to give us all the available information, there may be no way we can know that that is happening.

4. *They make the simple seem complex and incomprehensible.*

This technique often overlaps with the use of jargon, as in this case:

In Chapter 1, I mentioned that the term *auditory processing deficit* (APD) is used to describe some learning disabilities. There is great disagreement among the experts about exactly what this means, how one tests for it, and so on, but the label suggests that something is wrong with the ears of the child who has such a deficit. Once you learn that such children do not behave in subnormal ways on regular hearing tests, it is hard to imagine what kind of ear-related thing might be going on. For years, parents of children given this diagnosis had told me how frustrated they were, because they just could not understand what it was that their children could not do and why they couldn't do it. Psychologist Gael MacPherson and I had noticed that children given the APD label seemed very distractible. We also noticed that they scored low on tests on which the questions were spoken rather than printed for children to read at their own speed. We reasoned that children who have trouble maintaining their attention on a particular question are more likely to score low on tests with spoken questions, because if something distracts them while a question is being asked, they may hear only part of the question or none at all. Or they may have to ask to have it repeated and thus lose points for taking a long time to answer. For her doctoral research, MacPherson gave a large number of tests of various kinds both to children who had been diagnosed as APD and those who had not.[8] Her tests showed that the children given the APD label were distractible but did not perform in any uniform or predictable ways on any of the other tests of thinking, achievement, or hearing. In other words, those called APD apparently do *not* have some kind of complicated, hard-to-comprehend problem with their hearing *per se*, but they are easily distracted. If questions were presented to them in written form, but for only one or two seconds, then they would probably score low on those tests, too, so their problem is not really "auditory," nor is it hard to understand.

Many lawyers have a similar knack for making the simple seem complex and incomprehensible:

> My uncle, Bill Karchmer, was a lawyer, and from him I learned that some lawyers tell prospective clients, "You mustn't try to handle this case yourself. You really need to be represented by a lawyer." They portray the legal-judicial system as far too complicated for a layperson to understand. In fact, however, it is not so much that the system and the issues are too complicated for us laypeople to understand; instead, it is that courts are supposed to operate strictly according to certain rules of procedure, and cases can be lost simply because they are handled by someone who is unaware of those rules. This is not to say that laypeople with an impending court case should drop everything and thoroughly learn the rules of procedure; it is rather to say that we should not assume that the legal system is so far beyond our comprehension that we should not try to understand it and should not ask our lawyers to explain what they are doing and why.

5. *They present Ideas and Opinions as though they were indisputable Truths.*

As Studs Terkel notes, experts who are not all-wise can become all-powerful by asserting that they know the truth:

> "Twenty-five years ago, gerontologists said the way to successfully age was to disengage," and therapists based their work with older people on that assumption.[9] If you were old and unhappy, you were failing to do what you were *supposed* to do: withdraw from life gracefully.

Terkel was right, for even recently, I've heard therapists say that patients who became very withdrawn as they aged were simply behaving normally and needed no help or support.

Although it is extremely difficult to prove any single explanation of a person's behavior is true, psychotherapists often present their explanations as though they were true rather than as the educated guesses or even unfounded theories they really are:

> A therapist tells a sixty-five-year-old man who has recently become sexually impotent that impotence is caused by having had an intrusive, smothering mother during one's childhood. In one such case, the therapist knew that the man had just lost his job as top executive of a manufacturing company and had never been impotent before that time. The therapist's rigidity and arrogance about his view of the truth inhumanely delayed the patient's recovery, because it led down wrong paths in treatment.

This story also illustrates the tendency for stereotypic beliefs—in this case, that mothers are responsible for everything bad that happens to their offspring—to be presented as truths.

Although universities are thought to support academic freedom and promote learning from various viewpoints, academics are often bound by rigid ideas about their own field. Those in authority in academia often present their *opinions* about what belongs in their field as though they were indisputable, as in this example:

> When I was a sophomore English major, I was required to write a major essay about a piece of literature, and I chose to focus on the nature of the relationship between Huckleberry Finn and the slave Jim in Mark Twain's *The Adventures of Huckleberry Finn*. The instructor wrote that the paper was well done, but her concern was that it wasn't really a literature paper because it was "psychological." Papers about rodent imagery in Shakespeare and "s" sounds in Wordsworth's poetry were considered by the faculty in the English department at that time to be acceptable topics for "real" analyses of literature, but an exploration of the relationship between two characters was not. The key point here is not that this teacher had a *preference* or a set of *values* for judging what was acceptable but rather that she did not make it

clear that it was only her preference and her values. She wrote her comments in such a way that the standards she invoked seemed absolute, unquestionable. I have to admit that, in a sense, she foretold the future, because I became a psychology professor, not an English professor, but when I read her feedback on my paper, I felt at that time and for many years afterward that I had not been smart enough to understand what "real" literary criticism should be.

The arena of weight loss draws millions of desperate people to it, seeking help. It is demoralizing—and it promotes self-blame—when weight-loss experts confidently proclaim, "*This* is the way that *you* can lose weight" and turn out to be wrong. They, too, often present opinion as though it were truth:

Nearly everyone who has ever tried unsuccessfully to lose weight and keep it off has been told by doctors and other professionals, "The only way to lose weight is to eat less and exercise regularly." I recently told my physician that I felt my energy had for years been lower than it should be for someone my age, and that I felt that the extent of my weight problem was causing me chronic back pain. He told me that because I was forty-five years old, I couldn't expect to have as much energy or to weigh what I used to. He said in no uncertain terms that the only thing I could do was to eat less. "But I don't eat that much," I told him, "and whenever I eat less than usual, my energy level drops even lower!" He smiled, shrugged his shoulders, and ushered me out. A few days later, only half-believing that my doctor's opinion was absolute truth, I mentioned that discussion to my nutritionist, Carola Barczak. Carola recommended Elaine Gottschall's book, *Food and the Gut Reaction*, and from that book, I learned that some people cannot digest any grains at all, nor potatoes, chickpeas, sprouts, sugars, and a few other things.[10] Without reducing the amount of food I ate, I went off the items in Gottschall's list, and on the very first day, my energy level surged dramatically. My weight also slowly started to go down, taking pressure off my back after years of pain. My well-meaning doctor had simply conveyed to me the supposedly scientific theory that he had learned to treat as fact: Calories are the key, and everyone who cuts down on their calories can control their weight. However, recent research shows that there are sizable "individual differences in what the body does with unneeded calories: some people tend to store them as fat, others lay them down as muscle. Since building lean tissue uses up much more energy than storing fat, fat makers grow fat, while muscle makers stay trim. . . . The findings come from an experiment [reported in the *New England Journal of Medicine*] performed at Laval University in Quebec City in 1988 and 1989. Doctors put 12 pairs of identical twins on diets during which they ate 1,000 more calories a day than they needed, and they got almost no exercise. When it started, all were slim men in their early 20s with no family history of obesity. After 84 days, they had all eaten 84,000 excess calories," but some had grown fat, while others stayed relatively trim, the weight gains ranging from 4 to 13 kilograms. The study's director, Dr. Claude Bouchard, concluded, "The individual differences are amazing. They are huge. . . . Almost 40 per cent of the weight gain is explained by the propensity to store in the form of lean or fat tissue."[11]

Because many authorities regularly warn divorced mothers that their children will probably have significant emotional problems, such mothers listen anxiously to what therapists and clergy say. When the authorities' advice is handed down as though it is absolute truth, then, it matters desperately to many women:

Often, mental health professionals and members of the clergy have been quick to tell divorced mothers never, under any circumstances, to say anything negative about their children's fathers. They offer this advice as though it were undoubtedly in the children's best interests. As a result, even when a father routinely ignores or mistreats his children, the mother feels she must watch helplessly and in silence as her children decide that it must be *their own* failings that lead him to behave in that way. I do not advocate frequent trashing of an ex-spouse, but I do worry when people of authority present such guidelines as though they were absolute and applied throughout your child's life, without considering the devastating effects they could have on your child.

6. *They do not tell you all your options.*

How frustrating it is to work full-steam ahead and worry intensely about what we are doing, believing this is the best or only way to do it, only to learn that there were other, easier options—but that no one told us:

> The students in a doctoral program in psychology were becoming increasingly anxious about their upcoming "comprehensive examinations," which were to cover all of their course work. Each student worked steadily on her or his own, fighting off the rising feelings of panic and wondering how to review and absorb so much material. Just by chance, one of them learned from a recent graduate of the program that it would not be considered weakness, unprofessional behavior, or cheating if they studied in groups, each person reviewing and presenting a portion of the material. The graduate also revealed that copies of all previous comprehensive examinations were available on request from the program chairperson's secretary. The faculty had not intended to make the students' lives unduly difficult. Theirs was an unintentional omission, a simple failure to stop and think, to put themselves in the students' places; but the effect on the students was terribly unnerving.

It is especially upsetting when the consequences of a parent's limited awareness of possible courses of action are hurtful to a child:

> Bruno and Mary had divorced, and Bruno had moved to a neighboring country with their twelve-year-old son, Earl, while Mary stayed in the home where they had raised the child. For various reasons, Bruno had legal custody of the boy, but there had been no acrimonious dispute about that. Earl had a great deal of trouble adjusting to the new environment but had been very happy and had had many friends when living in the family home where he had spent the previous eight years. On a visit to his mother, Earl told her how miserable he was and how he longed to move back with her, go back to his old school, and be with his old friends. As they talked, they learned they had both been calmly assured by Bruno several times that he would not object if Earl chose to live with Mary. But when Mary phoned to inform Bruno that Earl wanted to stay on, Bruno exploded in a

rage and ordered her to send Earl back the next day as planned. Worried about Earl's depressed psychological state, Mary phoned a woman who was said to be a superb family lawyer and asked for an immediate appointment. The lawyer informed Mary that she had two options: to send Earl back to his father as originally scheduled *or* to go to court right away and ask for interim custody of Earl and schedule a full custody hearing later on. In view of Earl's emotional condition, Mary felt she had no choice but to follow the second option, and when the judge granted her interim custody and set a date for the full custody hearing, Mary forthrightly phoned Bruno and told him what she had done. He was so furious that she had asked for and received interim custody that he secretly planned and executed an elaborate arrangement to kidnap Earl and bring him home. After lengthy court proceedings in the foreign country, as well as vast financial and emotional expenses, Mary learned that the lawyer had neglected to mention a third option. She could have simply kept Earl and officially informed her ex-husband of that, without asking for interim custody, and then asked for a full hearing later on. Although Bruno might still have flown into a rage and arranged the subterfuge, it is possible that the less dramatic option might have resulted in less emotional and financial drain. In any case, as the client, Mary had the right to be informed of *all* of her options, but the lawyer did not do so. And when it was all over and Mary asked her lawyer why she had not mentioned that third option, the lawyer looked genuinely surprised and said, "Oh, didn't I mention that?" Like people in any line of work, some lawyers are more thorough and better able than others to consider what their clients know and do not know. But it is, after all, the lawyer's job to inform the client about all options.

7. *They tell you to leave it to them, because they are the experts.*

Most people have been told at some time to keep quiet or withdraw a request because they don't know what's good for them—or for others. In the following example, the people in power wanted me to let them decide on the best way for me to learn.

When I was in graduate school in clinical psychology, each student was required to take one "psychotherapy conference." This meant attending a once-a-week therapy session conducted by a professor, which the students observed through a one-way mirror. I had been assigned to a psychotherapy conference in which the patient was a child, and I asked to attend an additional one in which the patient was an adult, in order to learn more. The faculty in charge told me that they simply would not allow me to do that, that in their judgment it was not a good idea, and they would not tell me why. I upset them by pressing for an explanation, and they finally said, "If we let you do that, we'd have to let *everyone* do it"—a pretty lame reason, because there weren't many of us in the program anyway, there was plenty of room behind the one-way mirrors, and I couldn't find anyone besides myself who wanted to take a second conference. The main point, though, was that they resisted even offering an explanation, preferring to hide behind their positions as authorities.

Those in power frequently reassure people they are supposed to serve that their needs will be met, without thinking about how the decisions they make will affect their consumers' daily lives:

Benjamin was a young man who suffered from many food allergies that brought on asthmatic attacks and severe eczema, and on moral grounds he had become a vegetarian. During high school, he and his family had become accustomed to taking his food needs into account when they shopped and cooked. Just before enrolling in a private college where he was required to eat in the college's dining halls for his first year, Benjamin contacted the food service director. Benjamin described the restrictions on his food intake and said he was afraid that he wouldn't be able to find much to eat in the cafeteria offerings. The director assured him that there would be no problem. "Just leave it to me," he said, "since we know all about food allergies, and we cater specially to vegetarians." When Benjamin's first semester began, he found that the college offered only one vegetarian main dish at each meal, and it almost always included either dairy products or wheat, two of Benjamin's most severe food allergies. The cold salads that he could eat usually included wilted lettuce that was brown at the edges and tomatoes just this side of rotting. Starving after a couple of weeks of this diet, Benjamin went back to the food services director and reminded him, "You had said to leave it to you, but there is almost nothing here that I can eat. Would you please refund my food money for the rest of the year, so that I can buy and prepare food that I *can* eat?" The director refused his request and also did nothing to help.

8.   *They call it what it isn't.*

This technique can be a blatant distortion of the truth. In one such example, a doctor blithely told the family of a middle-aged man that the patient was "definitely conquering his cancer," when he had no justification for making such a claim (the patient, incidentally, died a month later). Such blatant distortions can be harmful because they conceal danger or the imminence of death behind masks of innocuous-sounding terms. The danger of less blatant distortions is that they can be harder to recognize, often because they come from some respected field of science or intellectual theory—such as psychoanalysis in the following examples:

> Because of the great respect so long accorded to Sigmund Freud, many men have been unfairly mortified by having their fears of being hurt or losing power mistakenly called "castration anxiety." Similarly, a great many women have had their wishes to achieve and to obtain some degree of influence and power mistakenly called "penis envy." More recently in the U.S. presidential election, Ross Perot called the responsible, professional, persistent questioning of him by two women interviewers on NBC television their attempts to "prove their manhood."

Calling something what it isn't often involves applying red-flag words to something that is not actually dangerous, as in this example:

> Many women, and many people of both sexes who are not white, have told me how uneasy they have been when hired in a workplace that has an affirmative action policy. The reason for their discomfort is that those who oppose affirmative action assert that its fundamental principle is "reverse discrimination," or lowering

the standards for hiring and promoting those who are not white, male, and able-bodied. There is, of course, a world of difference between lowering standards, on the one hand, and, on the other, actively seeking qualified candidates who are not white, male, and able-bodied. (It is worth noting that women and people of both sexes who are disabled or are not white have often actually had to be *more* qualified and *harder-working* than white, able-bodied males to be hired or promoted.) Furthermore, opponents of affirmative action tend not only to call it what it is not but also to call pre-affirmative action days what they were not; that is, they do not describe those earlier days as an era of the almost exclusive favoring of white, able-bodied men for hiring and promotions, a kind of affirmative action for them.

9. *They claim that what you want them to do is not their responsibility.*

What happens to the client or consumer when those charged with taking responsibility do not feel comfortable doing so and try to palm it off on someone else?

It's always been my understanding that it is the responsibility of judges to make decisions about thorny issues that come before them. The *Random House Dictionary*'s definition of *judge* is "A public officer authorized to hear and determine causes in a court of law; a magistrate charged with the administering of justice."[12] But when I told a conference of judges and lawyers that Jeffery Wilson's and my research had revealed rampant biases among professionals who do child custody assessments, one of the more senior jurists stood up during the question period and asked how judges could possibly make decisions in these cases if they couldn't rely on the therapists' recommendations. I thought that it was charmingly honest but alarming for a respected judge to feel uncomfortable shouldering the responsibility that judges are paid to shoulder.

It is especially problematic and frustrating when the person described as responsible is inaccessible:

Nurses cannot legally prescribe and order medication for patients. In theory, when a patient is in pain, the nurse can phone the doctor at home but is often in reality discouraged by some doctors' angry responses when they are called there. And in the whole range of institutions, how often are we told by the people on duty that they are not empowered to make the decisions we need to have made—but that the supervisors who *do* have that power are in meetings of unpredictable length, are out of the office, or are on vacation? As Rounds notes, "Conflicts often come to a head between nurses and residents over the issue of medication. The nurses aren't credentialed to prescribe medications. But because they spend all day and all night observing patients, they grow to learn what medication a patient should have and how much."[13]

10. They blame you for what is not your fault.

How many of us as parents have heard on interview night from our child's teacher that our child is behaving badly and that the misbehavior must be due to something we are doing or failing to do? When that happened to me, I learned that other parents had heard similar concerns from the same teacher, but we later learned that the teacher's husband had recently deserted her and their child, and she was dealing with her depression by yelling at the children in her class. And social worker Ben Carniol writes that social workers, whose work originated in the wish to support the poor and needy, are often quick to blame their clients: "In practice, rather than objectively empathizing and refraining from judgement, social workers [and other professional helpers] more likely attach 'blame.' "[14] Indeed, blaming is an especially common technique in all systems. Johnston's following observation about physicians applies to a wide range of authorities:

> "Belief in the importance of patient compliance allows for the blaming of the victim since, [*sic*] those who do not adhere to the advice of the lordly physician may be viewed as irresponsible, ignorant, and guilty. In addition, by withholding information, physicians maintain control and authority, the interruption of work routine is prevented, the inadequacies and failures of the health care providers are masked, and finally, the professional stance of detachment is protected."[15]

And we have all had an experience of being blamed for what is not our fault:

> When your new television or washing machine stops working, there is a good chance that the employees at the store where you bought it will insist that *you* must have done *something* to break it. I've been asked more times than I care to count whether I might have kicked a major appliance or dropped a heavy object on it.

As with other techniques, it is particularly daunting when the force of science or professional terminology is invoked in blaming the person for what is not her fault:

> In a highly publicized case, psychiatrist Margaret Jensvold had been hired to do research on "premenstrual syndrome" in a laboratory at the U.S. National Institute of Mental Health. When she asked to attend a conference on PMS that her male peers in the laboratory had been told they could attend, her request was denied. One man in the laboratory even told her that when he was at her professional stage, he had known nothing about PMS, so why should she? When she asked for a parking permit, she was accused of having an inflated sense of entitlement, of unjustifiable expectations. Her boss told her she didn't act dependent enough, and for all these reasons he ordered her to get psychotherapy. When he gave her a list of therapists from which she should choose, she went to the first one on the list— and much later learned that her boss was also *his* boss. Feeling understandably worried about this, she repeatedly asked the therapist whether or not he would keep confidential what she told him. He not only refused to give her that standard assurance but recorded on her file that she had made that request and was therefore "paranoid." He also said that her unhappiness in the laboratory was due to her "self-defeating personality disorder," a diagnostic category (at that time approved by the American Psychiatric Association) indicating a conscious or unconscious need or wish to be unhappy.

When we turn to authorities for help because we are already struggling to cope with some trouble, it is so disappointing to be treated as though we were to blame for that trouble. A farmer named Carroll Nearmeyer told Studs Terkel about how his banker blamed him for problems that had not been of his own making:

> When problems started coming up, I went to talk to my banker. I knew him personally and he knew me. But he had pressure from up above and so he was putting the pressure on me. He was trying to convince me I was a bad manager and for me to come home and write up a sale bill, list everything, and sell out. If I did that, I could pay them off and they, therefore, would not have had the pressure from up above. Being's as I'm a fourth-generation farmer, I wasn't about to just come home and sell out.
>
> They come at us with, You gotta have a cash flow, you gotta do a better job on your bookkeeping, a better job on your farming. But still when you sell that bushel of corn for less money than you produce it, you can only cut so far. Our taxes kept going up, interests kept going up on us. At one time, I was paying eighteen percent interest on my farm notes. I came up more short on payments. If I don't make a go of it now, the Newton National Bank will take it.[16]

Frustrating though it can be when those in power block our efforts to obtain help by what they say and what they don't say, it can be even harder to deal with the disempowering things they do and don't do. Recognizing and dealing with the latter kinds of techniques tend to require a greater understanding of the system from which you are seeking help than the former. The following chapter is designed to assist you in recognizing when you're being stymied by what authorities and experts do and don't do.

3

What They Do and
What They Don't Do

Some of the techniques in this chapter overlap with each other and with techniques in Chapter 2. Many of the examples are very strong stuff, but they reflect what happens in the real world, and indeed it is because of such stories that I decided to write this book. Some of the incidents that follow seem so extreme that, when I recount them in lectures, I am asked whether I chose them for their shock value. I don't choose them for that reason. I choose them because I know that they are *not* uncommon. What is shocking is that the most egregious stories about authorities are *not* rare. If the disempowering techniques caused only fleeting feelings of irritation, powerlessness, or shame, it would not be so critically important to understand how we are being treated. But remember that seeing what has happened to others and feeling it resonate with our own maddening or devastating experiences is a fundamental first step toward recovering from such mistreatment. And remember that in Chapter 8 we shall look at what can help.

As you read these examples, you may find yourself thinking,

"If only the consumer had done X, those awful things wouldn't have happened." Although we can take steps to avoid *some* of these outcomes, I decided not to address them in this book. There are many fine publications, such as those by Ralph Nader and *Consumer Reports* magazine, that can help us become informed consumers. The purpose of this book, though, is different. It is to stress that we ought not to have to spend a great deal of time learning a system inside and out, finding out its loopholes, and identifying its limitations when the system is supposed to be there to serve us. We especially shouldn't have to do all that at a time when we are seeking help because we are already in a vulnerable, drained, or needy state. In other words, yes, there is much we *can* do, but if we focus too intensely on that, we lose sight of the fact that we ought not to have to protect ourselves from authorities who claim to be there to help us. For that reason, I say little before Chapter 8 about what the client could have done to avoid disaster. In Chapter 8 the kinds of suggestions I make are less about how to learn about and beat the system than about how to protect ourselves from self-blame when the system fails us—although some of the points in Chapter 8 may have the added benefit of helping us get more out of the system than we have until now.

As for Chapter 2, I suggest you take notes relating the following techniques to your specific experiences.

11. They fragment you as a person.

Sometimes the fragmentation happens because a single authority deals with only one aspect of your functioning or your body and fails to consider how the different aspects relate to one another. At other times, as in the medical and mental health fields, many professionals each "work on" and consider only one part or system at a time, not consulting together to try to make sense of what is happening to the whole of you and what you need as a fully functioning human being. The people in different systems tend to work in fragmented ways for various reasons, but the most common one is simply a lack of knowledge: Training in one field all too rarely involves training in other fields that might be related. In Arnie's case, for example, if the family doctor had known much—or had stopped to think— about the effects of coughing on muscles, about simple massage techniques for alleviating those effects, and about nondrug treatment methods, Arnie would have suffered far less.

Arnie developed severe bronchitis after a bout of influenza. His continual, racking episodes of coughing strained the muscles around his rib cage, and he was constantly exhausted from being awakened during the night by the need to cough. Trying to clear up the cough, his family doctor prescribed decongestants and antihistamines that made Arnie drowsy but did not reduce the coughing. Then he gave Arnie a series of antibiotics, which caused severe constipation and then painful rectal tearing but did not stop the coughing. Owing to his drug-induced sleepiness and exhaustion from the coughs and rectal pains, he was unable to do much work and became mildly depressed. Because of his strained chest muscles, he had trouble breathing. Neither he nor his physician realized that those muscles were strained, and the doctor decided that Arnie's breathing trouble, fatigue, and depression called for tranquilizers. Not only did these fail to alleviate any of the symptoms but they also intensified Arnie's depression. When Arnie told the doctor this, he instructed Arnie to stop the tranquilizers, neglecting to mention that if he did not *gradually* reduce the dosage, he wouldn't be able to sleep, owing to the medication's "rebound" effect. So Arnie lost still more sleep. Fortunately, he went to a massage therapist, who got rid of the breathing difficulty by working on the muscles of Arnie's rib cage. But not until he told the whole story to his friend Susan, a nurse, did anyone explain the course of events. Susan said that the breathing problem had resulted from the hard coughing having wrenched the muscles of Arnie's rib cage and chest. Now, he could breathe more easily, but the cough persisted. One day, he wandered into a health food store and told an eighty-year-old man who worked there about the symptoms. The man prescribed capsules of fenugreek (a spice used in curry dishes) to thin the mucous. Arnie took four of these capsules during the next few hours, spent 2 ½ hours coughing up thick phlegm, felt almost normal after that, and after four more days on fenugreek was completely cured—after three months of suffering.

Had Arnie's doctor recognized that he understood only certain things about the body, and had the massage therapist thought not just about Arnie's pulled muscles but also about what could help the cough that kept wrenching those muscles, Arnie might have recovered much sooner.

In Arnie's case, the fragmentation was of his body. In other cases, the harm comes from professionals' splitting off of the body from the emotions. This next example is about a young girl who was taken to a surgeon because she complained of recurrent stomach pains. The surgeon thought about her complaint in terms of the causes most familiar to him: possible problems in her body. Neglecting some well-documented causes of stomachaches, he failed to consider that intense fears, anxiety, or reaction to having been sexually abused could have led to her pains. The surgeon, Dr. Stearne, removed the girl's appendix.

> A few days after the surgery, Stearne mentioned to me that the eleven-year-old's postoperative pathology work had indeed shown a normal appendix. "She'll never get appendicitis now," he said, "and besides that, I probably cured her symptoms of abdominal pain. She feels I took out what was wrong."[1]

When asked if he knew anything about her family life, the surgeon said he didn't know much. As a result of Dr. Stearne's fragmentation of this child into body and feelings, he subjected her to unnecessary surgery, and the real causes of her pain were ignored and untreated.

Here is another case of mind-body fragmentation I know about firsthand:

> A friend phoned me recently from the hospital. "I'm on a kidney dialysis machine at this very moment," she announced. It seems that her psychiatrist, forgetting about her body, had put her on the drug lithium to control her mood swings and failed to monitor the medication's side effects. As a result, she now has severe kidney trouble.

In arenas other than medicine, the impact of fragmentation has different consequences, but those consequences can nevertheless be distressing:

A private unemployment adviser told Jack, a forty-nine-year-old man who had just lost his job with his employer of thirty years, that he needed to draw up a good resume and start answering classified ads, without finding out whether the man had any self-confidence about job interviews, what was happening in his personal life, or whether he was in good physical health. Having paid the adviser $250 for his assessment, Jack assumed that the advice he had received should be all he would need. It had not occurred to Jack to ask about the adviser's training, which had dealt specifically with teaching people how to prepare resumes but had included nothing about understanding psychological factors relevant to searching for jobs. Jack put together his resume and began to answer advertisements. However, he had become so disheartened by losing his job that he had withdrawn emotionally from his wife, and she had moved in with their daughter and son-in-law. Feeling rejected and abandoned, Jack stopped eating properly and as a result became physically sluggish and depressed and did not present well when prospective employers looking for go-getters interviewed him.

Had Jack's adviser cared enough, or been taught well enough, to look at the whole picture of Jack's life, he could actually have helped his client.

12. They use outright fakery (either intentionally or not).

For the client who is misled or harmed by the fakery of experts, it doesn't much matter whether or not the fakery was intentional, because the harm has been done. If it was unintentional, however, some clients find it harder to get angry at the authority, and it can certainly be more difficult to hold the authority accountable or obtain compensation. A common cause of unintentional fakery is the authority's lack of information; after all, probably no physician, for instance, regularly reads every report of up-to-date research in every important medical journal. That doesn't stop some of them from acting as though they know everything: "As Zola (1978) has observed, the medical profession has claim over the label of illness and *anything* to which it may be attached, irrespective of its capacity to deal with it effectively."[2] But some professionals behave quite purposely in a fraudulent way. For instance, law professor Derrick Bell has written that, among lawyers, "Dishonesty is, if not rampant, sufficiently high to cause concern."[3]

The following story comes from the financial realm, whose authorities are not immune to fakery.

> Bob, a U.S. citizen who moved to Canada because of his job, sought help preparing his tax return after his first year in Canada. He specifically asked his accountant whether or not he needed to continue filing U.S. tax returns while living in Canada, and the accountant said, "That's absolutely unnecessary." After many years of filing only Canadian returns, Bob switched to a different accountant, who informed him that he should have been filing U.S. returns all along. And indeed, that was the year that the Internal Revenue Service wrote to ask Bob why he had not filed returns with them.

In Bob's case, his first accountant's confident way of misinforming him could have led to Bob's having to pay a substantial penalty. In the following story, the victim of fakery suffered significant physical consequences.

> A counselor in a weight-loss program advised a forty-year-old woman that, because she gained weight on a 1,000-calorie-a-day diet, if she cut back to 750 calories a day she would definitely lose weight. After becoming exhausted and ill by sticking to 750 calories a day for six weeks, the woman found a good nutritionist, who explained that *reducing* her food intake caused her to *gain* weight, because her body reacted as many bodies do to starvation, by holding on for dear life to whatever food she ate.

Sometimes, fakery has no easily identifiable consequences but generally erodes the credibility of experts. Such instances, like the one below, make it increasingly hard for the public to know which so-called experts speak with integrity and which do not.

> Marilyn's close friend, Deena, had been married for many years to a psychotherapist who, Deena discovered, had been having sex with many of his patients and with a few of Deena's friends. One day, Marilyn turned on the television and heard a maga-

zine-show host announce that Deena's husband was their regular advice giver. The first phone call from a viewer that day came from a woman who was despondent because her husband had been having an extramarital affair, and she wanted the psychiatrist to tell her what to do. Appalled, Marilyn telephoned the television producer's office. The producer was not in, so Marilyn told his secretary that she wanted him to know that the psychotherapist had acknowledged having many affairs himself and had also slept with his patients. The secretary replied, "Oh, the producer knows this." The producer was knowingly participating in this sham.

It seems particularly shocking when the consequences of fraudulence are dangerous to people's health or even life-threatening. Accordingly, it is worrying that, in 1986, when the Food and Drug Administration went back and checked drug studies that its agency had conducted for the previous ten years, nearly two hundred studies "contained so many flaws that the ability of the tested drugs to produce the claimed results was seriously questioned. About 40 studies exhibited recklessness or outright fraud."[4] The article in which the above report appeared also included the following information:

> Dr. Robert Slutsky, a promising young heart specialist at the University of California, San Diego, School of Medicine resigned in 1986 after officials there disclosed that he had committed "extensive research fraud" by making up data from experiments he had never conducted. . . . Investigators said 13 of his papers contained outright fraud and 55 were "questionable."[5]

Although we know that many researchers are honest, the key point here is that the public has no way of knowing which ones are and which are not.

13. They transform what you say into "proof" that you are bad, crazy, or wrong.

To justify not meeting our needs, institutions pathologize us, make it seem as if we are disturbed, crazy, bad, or wrong. This is all the more likely to happen when we object to the way we are treated and try to stand up for our rights. Gloria Steinem has written that the idea that an individual might have intrinsic worth is dangerous to authoritarian systems and so is condemned in a variety of ways, anything that puts the blame on the individual.[6] This technique is often used when the people who could meet our needs either don't want to or through no fault of their own *cannot* meet them. In both of the following examples, the technique was used purposefully and aggressively.

> As mentioned earlier, the problems of farmers have brought them up against many uncaring authorities, and some authorities disempower them through negative labeling. One such man told Studs Terkel: "Then I got involved with this farm group, and there is people just like me. They get tagged as radicals right away. 'Cause we're supposed to be civilized now. It's all right for some S.O.B. in a white shirt and tie to come along and take our farms away from us on paper. But it's not all right for us to try to keep him from doin' that. The minute we say we're not gonna let him do that, we become radicals."[7]

The case of the woman psychiatrist who was told she was to blame for the harassment to which she was subjected was mentioned in Chapter 2. She was also the subject of offensive labeling:

> When psychiatrist Dr. Margaret Jensvold was working in a research laboratory at the National Institute of Mental Health, her boss kept her from participating as fully in the work and having as many opportunities as her male peers in the laboratory. When she objected to this treatment, he justified it by telling her, among other things, that she wasn't dependent enough in her behavior toward him. And when she requested a parking permit, she was criticized for having too great a sense of entitlement.

14. They are unwilling to listen to you.

An authority's failure to listen to a client can be devilishly hard to pinpoint, but the client may sense it because of the way their eyes glaze over or because of the dawning awareness that the authority is forgetting key information the client has provided. Maggie Kuhn, founder and leader of the Gray Panthers, calls this technique "a gross misuse of power."[8] Pretending to listen, but then ignoring what you have said, is a variation on this theme.

> Before Kyle discovered a wonderful automobile mechanic, he described, to a series of mechanics at different garages, the way his car engine on occasion made a loud, knocking sound. This worried Kyle, because he was about to take the car on a long trip. Each mechanic in turn phoned to explain in a patronizing way that he hadn't heard a thing the one time he took it for a five-minute test drive. Each had clearly failed to take in Kyle's report that it happened only intermittently.

In that example, had the experts listened, they would not only have helped Kyle but they might even have made some money by finding that the car needed repair and then fixing it.

In the next example, the unheard information concerned not machines but important family relationships:

> A wife and husband sought help from a parenting-advice program when they learned that their teenaged son had become a heavy drinker of alcohol. The counselor who "facilitated" the parents' group to which they were assigned told them they needed to be "absolutely strict and firm" with their son. They replied that they had always been that way, because they both felt that discipline and clear limits were important for children and adolescents. The group leader responded, "You really must be absolutely firm." They felt terrible, because the leader's response implied that they hadn't "really" tried what he was suggesting. Because, in their experience, that approach had failed, they were left feeling helpless and hopeless, not knowing what to try next. And added to those upsetting feelings was the feeling that they were neither heard nor believed.

Because part of the clergy's role is to be caring, it can be especially hard (and painful) to recognize when members of that community fail to listen to us or ignore what we have said, as I illustrate in the next two stories:

A man had joined a particular synagogue partly because he had been told it was "a warm, welcoming community." After he had been a member for many years, within one six-week period someone very close to him died, and his long-standing common-law relationship ended, but he heard from almost no one in his congregation, including the rabbi. Thinking that perhaps those whom he had considered close friends must not have heard the news, he contacted several of them and was devastated to learn that they had known but simply hadn't bothered to call. Of these, only one made any subsequent attempt to see him or offer comfort, although when all had asked how he was doing, he had acknowledged that he was having a rough time. When he told the rabbi how much this treatment had hurt him, the rabbi ignored his statement that he had explained his situation to the congregants and said merely, "You must have given them the message that you were doing just fine and didn't need their support. You really do appear to be a very self-sufficient man, you know."

He was devastated and felt abandoned by his community and his rabbi.

Many women have told me of going to their clergy in great distress because their husbands were physically abusing them. In some cases, the abuse was unusually severe, such as men who forced their wives to have sex with other men in front of them. According to these women, some clergy (regardless of religion or religious denomination) wouldn't even let them tell their stories. Instead, as soon as the women mentioned abuse, they interrupted to say, "You shouldn't talk this way about your husband. After all, you promised before God to be loyal to him, and God wants you to obey him, no matter what he does."

Such women feel powerless to escape from their abusive situations, especially if they are devoutly religious and therefore feel they must do as their religious leaders instruct them. After such treatment, then, in addition to being subjected to sexual abuse by their husbands, they must cope with feeling let down by their clergy.

15. They simply do not answer your questions, or they may refuse outright to answer them.

Some experts and authorities are quite skilled at pretending to listen and then seeming to answer your questions. When you interact with them in person, you may find that you don't realize until after your encounter that they did not reply to your queries. When the interaction is on paper, it tends to be no less frustrating but it is easier to spot this failure.

> A very bright university student wanted to be excused from taking two required courses for his major, because his high school education in another country had covered that material in great depth. The four letters that he had sent to the chairperson of his department and to the dean of the college brought no reply, and he was left not knowing whether to go ahead and enroll for more advanced, challenging courses—at the risk of not being allowed to graduate because of not having taken the required ones—or to take the lower-level ones that were required.

This was a particularly stark instance of an authority completely failing to respond to queries.

When a loved one is seriously ill, or when our children are having problems in school, we often feel caught in a bind about asking questions of those who have the power to help—or hurt—us or our loved ones. We worry that if we ask questions, the doctor cannot answer or does not wish to take the time to explain, or if teachers think we are questioning their handling of our child, they will take out their irritation with us on the innocent, vulnerable party.

> Mark's uncle lived alone and was undergoing chemotherapy for cancer. The uncle was reluctant to "bother" his doctor by asking "too many" questions. When accompanying him to the doctor, Mark had a number of concerns but wanted to respect his uncle's wish to avoid taking too much of the doctor's time. So he wrote out several questions and asked the nurse to give them to the doctor before he saw his uncle. When the doctor came to examine him, he did so hastily and started to leave. Mark said,

"Excuse me, doctor, but did you have a chance to look at my note?" He looked peeved, rapidly addressed two of the questions Mark had written, and left. He never replied to Mark's concerns about his uncle's continuing headaches or the hand tremor that showed up when he tried to write.

Chapters 5, 6, and 7 are about the importance of questioning authorities, but as we see in this example, even if we summon up the courage to ask questions, the authority may still avoid answering them.

16. They intimidate you.

Threats of lawsuits and labeling with damning names are two of the most common, but certainly not the only, forms of intimidation.

> Elaine, who suffered physical problems from working in a sealed building (Technique 3), learned from a sick building syndrome specialist that the building's owners informed him that, when they were required to do laboratory analyses of the air in the building, they had it purified first. Then, the owners used the results of the analyses as "proof" that nothing was wrong with the building, that the people who were complaining were simply suffering from job stress. When Elaine wrote a memo to her bosses to report this information, saying she was concerned about the workers' health and about the phenomenally high rent being paid to the developers who owned the building, her bosses showed the memo to the building's owners. The owners promptly had their lawyers send her a letter on embossed stationery, threatening to sue her for libel. They never did clean up the building, however.

> Marianne had fought for equal pay and high-quality child care in her workplace, and for her pains she was negatively labeled by her employer as a "power-hungry man-hater who just wants to cost us a lot of money and doesn't want to take responsibility for her children."

17. They do a little but pretend they have done a lot.

When we turn to authorities or experts for help, few of us know much about what resources, tools, or powers are available to them. As a result, we may not know when they have failed to do a proper job, as the couple in this story learned too late:

> Dr. Hart, a psychologist, was asked to do a thorough assessment in a child custody dispute. After conducting the assessment, he recommended that the children live with their father and stepmother, and one of his reasons was that those adults were more intelligent than the mother and stepfather and therefore were better able to take care of the unusually bright children. However, although Dr. Hart had interviewed the four adults, he had done no intelligence testing whatsoever and therefore was not in a position to make claims about who was the more intelligent. The mother and stepfather had known that tests could be used to assess children's intelligence but did not learn until well after the custody hearing that there are tests for adults' intelligence as well.

It is especially true that when we are in reduced circumstances or weakened condition, we may feel grateful for small benefits and believe we are too powerless or fragile to fight for any more consideration. This is all the more so when the person or group handing out the crumbs acts as though it were a whole cake:

> Although some older Americans have simply been pleased by "senior citizens' discounts" given by a number of business establishments, others have a different view of how our society treats its older members: "You couldn't care less about Golden Buckeye discounts. Old people get fifteen or twenty percent off. I call that novocaine. They give that to old Americans instead of a guaranteed annual wage or a decent pension system. They numb us with a few little goodies."[9] A recently retired but quite frail widow had just moved to a retirement home where she was primarily confined to a single small room. Her social worker told her that she should feel happy because now she could get senior citizens' discounts for movies and travel. What no one informed her was that, if her late husband's pension could have been

transferred to her when he died, or if any level of government had provided sufficient funds, she could have afforded a part-time helper and remained in the apartment where she had lived for decades.

This inability to speak of things only vaguely thought of—what seem to be the "impossibles"—truly relegates such possibilities to the realm of the impossible.

18. They behave irresponsibly, immorally, or even viciously.

Irresponsible or immoral behavior may be unintentional, of course, but viciousness is harder to rationalize in that way. Service station attendants who cry out in alarm, "I hope you don't intend to drive this car while the oil is so low!" when they know perfectly well it is *not* low are using this technique. In the following example, as in many other cases, it is hard to know whether or not the department chairperson who hired the man really believed the advice he gave him and whether or not he recanted out of fear or out of a conscious wish to impede his progress. In any case, the damage to his career was considerable:

> Scott was a junior member of a university faculty who had been hired on a three-year contract. He was told that at the end of that time, his contract could be renewed for another three years if his performance was good enough. At the time he was hired, he asked the man who chaired his department what would be considered "good enough" and received the reply that his primary focus should be on teaching his undergraduate courses and that "of course, you should try to do some research as well." But the department head explicitly emphasized Scott's teaching responsibilities. At the end of Scott's three-year term, his contract was not renewed, and the evaluation committee explained that this was because he had failed to carry out and publish much research. When he protested that he had been concentrating on his teaching and had received excellent course evaluations from his students and had created two popular new courses, the committee said that this was not nearly as important as research. In response, Scott reported what the depart-

ment chair had said at the time he was hired, but the head flatly denied ever having made such a statement.

When I heard the next story, although I was shocked by how starkly the psychiatrist's immorality—and even viciousness— came through, I was not surprised by the content of his advice, because I have frequently heard therapists express such beliefs about what constitutes appropriate "treatment" or what patients really need.

> A psychiatrist agreed to see a heterosexual couple who came to him for help with their marital problems. He asked first to speak to both members of the couple together and then to each one separately. When he met with them together, he simply listened while the wife said that she considered her husband insensitive to her need for affection and warmth before sex and had some- times tried to force her to have sex with him, even to the point of using physical coercion. The husband said he felt that his wife was not sufficiently interested in sex. When the husband left the therapist's consulting room, the psychiatrist advised the wife to try to be more responsive to her husband's sexual needs. When the wife then left the room and the psychiatrist saw the husband alone, he advised him to "just fuck someone else."

If the husband genuinely wanted to save his marriage, that advice was no help, but if he followed it, his wife was betrayed by both her therapist and her husband. In any case, the psychi- atrist's conduct clearly came from his own needs and bizarre attitude, not from any wish to help his clients.

In the medical realm, a surgeon told me he always uses a general rather than a local anesthetic, because he likes to get rough when he operates. He denied having said that after I filed a complaint against him. But as a result of this experience, I wasn't surprised to read Mark Kramer's description of anoth- er surgeon's conduct at the end of an operation to remove a tumor in the patient's lower bowel:

> Job done. He closes quickly. He sutures the scar with monofila- ment. He helps the very good technician undrape the patient. When he comes to the penis, he pauses and regards it. It's point- ed chinward, taped, a catheter emerging from its tip.

"You want to see an example of passive aggression?" he asks. He yanks the adhesive off the penis, perhaps more forcefully than is necessary.

"There," he says. "Now I don't have to go home and kick the dog."[10]

19. They support other people in their system instead of helping you.

This practice is discussed in Chapter 4, but it is worth saying here that some authorities consciously choose to support their system rather than the consumer, but others are so caught up in the system's daily operation that they do not pull back and consider how it affects the client. They may even lose sight of the fact that their system might have been established for the benefit of the client.

> When I worked at a government-funded clinic assessing delinquent teenagers, I noticed that, in order to avoid mockery and ostracism at school, a goodly number of these youths had stolen clothes or makeup that they could not afford. I raised this issue in a clinic meeting, pointing out that many of the families we saw were terribly impoverished and perhaps the best help we could give them would be to try to arrange for them to receive additional financial assistance or help in finding jobs that paid decent wages. Because our workplace was a mental health setting and not an agency that could give money directly to our patients, I was told that we should restrict our work to psychological assessment and therapy, that it was "not part of our mandate" to focus on financial need. In order to protect the traditional limitations of mental health work, we were to don blinders and ignore the real needs of the people we were supposed to serve. I felt frustrated and saddened to see how our clients' welfare took a backseat to empty protocol.

In the next story, a college student was stunned to find that the university employee who was supposed to be her primary source of help felt that her responsibility to a co-worker took precedence over her responsibility to the student:

A mature woman college student was sexually harassed by one of her male professors. She reported this to her institution's sexual harassment officer, a woman who at first was understanding and emphatic, even saying that she had had similar experiences with the same man. However, at the end of the interview, the officer told the student, "I do sympathize with you because of what he has put you through, but if you ever tell anyone that, I'll deny having said it, because I'm going to need his support for something I am trying to do in part of my life that has nothing to do with my job as harassment officer."

In the following example, a police detective dealing with an assault charge chose to support the assailant's lawyer because he worked with the lawyer on many cases and on a committee:

A middle-aged, deeply disturbed woman assaulted a woman named Ms. Burks, who had done nothing to provoke the attack. The victim and a witness to the incident reported it to Detective Mallon, and he expressed concern and assured them he would charge the attacker with assault. After many weeks had passed, Ms. Burks phoned to ask Detective Mallon what was happening. He told her that he had been unable to serve the assailant with notice that she was being charged, because she would not answer the door at her home. Ms. Burks gave him the address where the woman worked, but six weeks later she still had not been served. Ms. Burks's lawyer later learned what accounted for Detective Mallon's slow pace: He and the assailant's lawyer had worked on cases together for twenty-five years and served together on a committee appointed by the mayor. As a result, Mallon had not wanted to jeopardize their relationship.

The fact that the victim appealing for help or justice may be very young and vulnerable does not prevent some powerful authorities from siding with those in their own system who have hurt her:

Dr. Wells, a psychiatrist who had for many years headed an intensive treatment center for emotionally disturbed teenagers, appeared in court when he was charged by a former patient with having repeatedly sexually assaulted her when she, at age 14, was his patient. In the course of the trial, Dr. Wells openly acknowledged that he had been addicted to drugs and alcohol and had also told the young patient, during the period of his sexual assaults on her, that his sexual contacts with her were improving his relationship with his wife. In spite of this clearly immoral, unethical, unprofessional behavior, a psychiatrist who had worked with him testified in court in support of Dr. Wells's good character.

20. They change the rules as they wish but pretend rules are absolute and unchangeable.

Some people in authority use this technique knowingly, too, but others become so absorbed in acting as they choose that they lose sight of the fact that they are changing the rules or making them up as they go.

> Ellen's experience (described in Chapter 1) with the unemployment officer exemplifies this technique: Although both the officer with whom she dealt and the one with whom her sister had dealt worked for the same agency, each presented his own personal preferences about how to proceed as though it were The Only Way to function in that agency—and as though those seeking help should have known which way to behave. The man who spoke to Ellen wanted her to tell the whole story on her own, but the man who spoke to her sister wanted her to speak only minimally and only in answer to his questions.

In the following example, Betty could hardly believe the arbitrary changes that took place before her eyes.

> In the graduate educational institution where she worked, Betty was chosen to represent students on an important committee. She had agreed to serve on the committee because she hoped to help make some changes for students and for women throughout the institution. For some reason that never became clear to her, during her second year on the committee, she was elected to be its chair, and so she believed that she would have some degree of power. But to her surprise, the truly powerful, higher-status, mostly male members of the committee kept changing the rules of procedure on the spur of the moment and insisting that she follow them. For example, during her first year on the

committee, she had watched as the man who was then chairing the meetings frequently said, "As chair I am not supposed to have a vote, so for now I'm not going to be chair, and I'll vote." He would physically switch to a different seat, cast his vote—which was often the deciding one—and then resume his former seat and his place as head of the committee. When Betty headed the committee and tried to do something similar to break a deadlock, the man who had been chair the previous year angrily told her she could not break the rules that way!

As most people would feel under such circumstances, Betty was confused and aghast. What compounded the difficulty for her was that the perpetrators of this injustice acted as though their behavior were perfectly reasonable and morally upright.

Having read through the techniques, you may wish to turn immediately to Chapter 8 to see what strategies people have found helpful in recovering from the techniques' ill effects. Or you may wish first to read the discussion in Chapter 4 about *why* authorities and experts use these techniques.

4

Why Do They Act That Way?

Some authorities, as well as representatives and employees of major institutions, intentionally make people whom they are supposed to help feel stupid and powerless, but others do so unintentionally and for a variety of reasons. Those who do it intentionally feel more powerful and capable when they make others feel the opposite—and tend not to worry much about the harm they are doing to those others. Consciously or unconsciously, they revel in the knowledge of their power, and they feel more secure in that knowledge every time they watch a help seeker squirm. We've all met people like that, and we may or may not be surprised to learn that they often rise to positions from which they knowingly mistreat others.

The reasons that other, better-intentioned people in positions of power use the techniques described in Chapters 2 and 3 are more complicated and more varied. For instance, as Glenna Atwood wrote in 1991, "I learned that doctors too are human: Some find it difficult to say, 'I don't know,' when they can't diagnose an illness. Some find it difficult to tell the patient

71

when they do know. Some are insensitive. All doctors are different, just as all patients are different."[1] Having been in authoritative positions in many institutions myself, I can describe some of those reasons based on firsthand experience. First of all, although they may not readily admit it, many people in such positions don't believe they have the right to be there. They feel that they lack the experience and the knowledge to do what they are expected to do. This set of feelings is so common that it has been given the label impostor syndrome.[2] As part of my training for my master's degree in psychology, I worked in a hospital clinic conducting detailed assessments of children who had school-related problems. I was twenty-three years old when I began that work, and my grades in classroom and interviewing courses had been good, but I felt stunned when I was suddenly expected to be an authority, to be able to help people, and to know more about them than they knew about themselves. Many of my classmates told me that they felt much the same way. This is no different from what happens to most students in the so-called helping professions, and something similar happens to people who are hired to work in other systems—law and the courts, education, banking, government agencies, and so on. You may have been trained by the best possible people, and your work may have been highly evaluated. You may have learned a substantial body of the knowledge that is considered essential in your field. But suddenly coming face-to-face with the patients/clients/consumers whom you and you alone are expected to help can be quite daunting. Worse still, it is likely that at no time in your training did any teacher or supervisor tell you how uncertain you would probably feel or what to do when those feelings arose.

In that situation, then, many of us have felt insecure, afraid of not doing well, of looking foolish, of not being able to help the people we are paid—and want—to help. Usually, at least initially, we deal with this dilemma by doing what we have been told by our teachers is the right way to proceed, the professional way to act, the method based on what they say has proven to work. In the best of cases, this means putting into action the helpful teachings from experts, but in worse cases, it means unquestioningly and uncritically carrying out orders or repeating the mistakes, distortions, and injustices of the past to cover our own insecurity. It also, at worst and not uncommonly, means identifying uncritically with powerful and arrogant models.

What others have done before us is often presented as the tried-and-true way to proceed, the result of a long history of accumulated knowledge and wisdom. Rarely do any of us in our prejob training, or our first years on the job, hear our trainers admit that they don't know an answer or that they don't know how to help those who come seeking assistance. Social worker Ben Carniol reports that a colleague told him:

> The thing is, the supervisor sometimes doesn't have the answer either. But instead of admitting it, the supervisor scares away the worker. After being treated that way, the worker learns not to ask again. Especially since it's the supervisor who evaluates the performance of the front-line worker.[3]

Similarly, it is highly unusual to hear supervisors acknowledge that the client/consumer might be right. Sadly, the tried-and-true ways most likely to survive are those that help protect the system and maintain its power. In most systems, the ethos that allows the system to resist change includes belief in the omniscience and omnipotence of those in power. If those in power are supposed to know everything and to be able to do anything, then *not* to know what to do can seem shameful, and *not* to be in control can seem a sign of danger and failure. Powerful people can convey with a raised eyebrow or a particular look the message that less powerful people in the system and the system's consumers had better not question what the system defines as the truth. Thus, because the system has different kinds of power over both groups, its employees and consumers are pressed to help perpetuate that definition, making it unlikely that the system will have to change.

A common and effective way that authorities avoid the risk of questioning the rightness of tradition is to find scapegoats; then, when they slip up, they blame someone else, and their position remains safe.⁴ The traditional teachings include warnings about consumers who expect the impossible, who are bent on destroying the system, who are constant sources of annoyance. In this way, insecure "helpers" or employees who feel inadequate to assist the client assume all too easily that the client fits into one of these problem categories. If the people at the very top don't frown on such scapegoating (or don't even acknowledge it) or on any of the disempowering techniques, chances are that no one will break the cycle. No one will question what is going on and the extent to which the system actually helps those it is supposed to serve.

Aside from those who crave power for its own sake, and beyond the general picture just described, there are other reasons that those with power or authority use disempowering techniques. I present them beginning roughly with those that involve the most selfish motives and generally move toward the less selfish, more sympathy-inspiring ones. At the end of this chapter, I deal with the question of whether people with certain types of motives tend to use particular techniques rather than others, but let me note here that in general, people's motives do not determine which techniques they use.

As you read through the range of motives, it might be useful to keep in mind that those authorities whose motives are toward the benign end of the spectrum are more likely to respond positively and helpfully if you point out to them that you are not getting the help you are seeking, or if you mention the specific disempowering techniques they have been using, or if you use some of the other strategies described in Chapter 8.

—*Some people (or their bosses) care most of all about money, efficiency, or avoiding ruffling the feathers of the powerful.* As Pilisuk writes, when executives make decisions about whether or not to recall products known to be dangerous, "In many cases, the risk to individual lives is judged acceptable and worth the benefits to 'society,' to the corporate bottom line, or to executive resumes."⁵ As I mentioned in Chapter 1, I never knew how destructive such people could be until I realized that the movie *Class Action* was based on manufacturers' actual practice of *not* recalling defective products when the estimated costs of legal settlements with victims are lower than the costs of recall.

—*Some people need to have total control.*[6] They either enjoy having total control over others or feel terrible, even frightened, if they do not. A famous American industrialist is reported to have conducted staff meetings standing on top of his desk in order to feel that sense of enormous power and to make clear to his staff that he was in control.[7] And this story comes from the healthcare system:

> Another horror story involved a newly diagnosed parkinsonian whose doctor had just prescribed Sinemet for her for the first time: one pill in the morning and one at night. Wary because she had had many bad reactions to medications in the past, she decided to start with only half a pill at a time to see how she might react. The half pill made her feel very ill, and so did each succeeding dose. She called her doctor to explain that the medication, even a half pill at a time, made her very ill. He responded, "I told you to take a whole pill. You do as I say; I am the doctor." He failed to tell her that a few people cannot tolerate Sinemet at all and that she might be one of them. Eventually he did take her off Sinemet, but only after he had established who was the boss.[8]

And some people who have enormous power simply don't give a damn about the consumer. A woman wrote to Ann Landers to say that her boss, a doctor, always arrived in his office an hour late. She said that he

> "sits at his desk, feet up, talking to his broker, his kids, his mother or a golf buddy for an hour" while people are waiting to see him. "If anyone complains about waiting, we've been instructed to say" he is consulting with a colleague. Sometimes, between appointments, he "goes to his desk to do accounting while people are waiting to see him. When he strolls in late because he overslept, we are told to say he was delayed in surgery."[9]

Mark Kramer has called this attitude "the miracle of insularity."[10]

—*Some people use disempowering techniques because they are given rewards that urge them to subordinate consumers' interests to their own.*

In a scandal involving a large auto repair chain, customers were told their cars needed repair even when they were in good condition. It turned out that the mechanics had been placed on an incentive program, so that they received commissions for the work they did—evidently, whether or not it was necessary.

Drug companies are known to offer perks—to the tune of $165 million one recent year—on gifts, dinners, and vacations to persuade doctors to use their products. Senate Labor and Human Resources Committee head, Sen. Edward Kennedy, remarked that "Patients have the right to expect that the prescription drug they are taking is medically appropriate . . . not part of their doctor's frequent prescriber vacation plan."[11]

—*Many people don't want to be seen to break the professional or corporate mold*. Sometimes, this is because they fear being fired or denied raises and promotions.

A man I knew had been hired by a major oil company, ostensibly to work on environmental protection. In the course of the job, he discovered that the company was seriously polluting the air and nearby waters and that he was given far too few staff and far too small a budget to enable him to reduce the pollution significantly. When neighbors of one of the refineries held a public meeting to complain about the filthy air and water, the environmental protection worker attended the meeting at his boss's request and defended the company's actions. To have done otherwise could well have meant he would be fired. From the public's point of view, this man seemed very powerful, but the truth was that his authority and resources were severely limited. Rather than resigning or raising a fuss about company policy, he dealt with his situation by remaining silent and continuing his work on his small window-dressing project, which helped conceal the environmental damage his corporation was doing.

Other times, people fear breaking the mold because they dread being considered wimpy (and often, for members of both sexes, not "man" enough). And sometimes they are afraid of their boss's or disciplinary body's views of nontraditional conduct. Therapists, for instance, often worry that their disciplinary body is more likely to convict them of unethical behavior when they diverge from tradition in trying to help clients than when they follow traditional practices, even when the latter are detrimental to their clients.

> A psychologist-in-training entered a meeting with her supervisor, saying, "I've done something terribly wrong with one of my patients, and I feel awful about it." When the supervisor asked what she had done that was so bad, the trainee said, "You know that eighteen-year-old woman I've been seeing? The one whose parents and siblings are all alcoholics? Well, she has spent most of her life taking care of them. She wants to go to junior college, but she has been so busy taking care of other people that she hasn't learned to make time to do things for herself. So, I gave her a calendar and helped her draw up a schedule: Monday, she will write to request an application from one school, Tuesday she will write to another school for an application form, etc." The supervisor asked why she thought that was wrong, and the trainee said, "All through graduate school, the psychologists who taught us said that we aren't supposed to *mother* our patients. We are supposed to act like blank screens, just listen to them talk, and occasionally interpret something they have said. So I know I did wrong." Fortunately, the supervisor assured her that helping set up a schedule was exactly what the patient needed, but the trainee was absolutely right in assuming that many of her colleagues would have said she had done wrongly.

Professionals' fear that untraditional conduct puts them at risk is justified by the decisions of many discipline committees in many professions. In view of this, it is ironic that, when it comes right down to it, those bodies tend to protect their own. As a lawyer friend of mine pointed out, his bar association typically disciplines only relatively powerless lawyers (and usually for only minor infractions), with just enough major convictions of powerful lawyers to be able to "prove" to the public and the government that it is holding its lawyers to ethical standards.

—*Often, people feel pressured to know it all.* An outgrowth of this pressure is that many people don't know that they don't know everything. Pilisuk writes, "No one thought ahead of time, Glendinning points out, that the Pinto car or the Dalkon shield would be dangerous."[12] Thus, many workers in major systems are trapped by the mistaken belief that experts know everything in their field.

A few years ago, I heard a prominent writer publicly blame herself for what seemed to be her daughter's serious emotional problems. I felt great sympathy for this woman and hated to see her taking on the entire responsibility, especially because I had heard nothing to suggest that it was warranted. During the discussion period, I suggested (with empathic intent) that mothers are quick to blame themselves and only themselves but that it sounded as though other people in the young woman's life and possibly some physiological factors might have contributed to her troubles. Apparently feeling that she ought to have had a complete command of the issue and that no one else ought to be able to see anything more, the writer became extremely defensive and angry, and years later, she refused to appear on a television show with me. Recently, however, she has publicly described the physiological basis that was discovered for her daughter's trouble, and now the writer has (not surprisingly) become an ardent advocate of the physiological approach.

A subcategory of the belief that experts know everything is the mistaken belief that experts know their own limitations, have an inkling of what they *don't* know, and will refer you elsewhere when they cannot help you. Usually, in fact, they do as those above them and those who preceded them have done, not stopping to ask themselves whether what they have to offer is what the consumer really needs.

All too often, neither the direct service provider nor the supervisor knows what the provider does not know. This phenomenon is so common and so important that it is covered in greater depth in Chapters 5 and 6, but here is one example:

Amazing though it may seem, Nazario reports that "Researchers say most students graduate from the nation's 126 medical schools without ever having a patient examination observed [by medical faculty]. When USC began systematically requiring such exams a few years ago, faculty members were appalled by what they saw. One student thumped a cardiac patient's chest with a medical hammer, and others didn't detect obvious heart murmurs and enlarged livers."[13]

—Some authorities use disempowering techniques because they feel overwhelmed. The system that feels monolithic, inhumane, and overpowering to consumers often feels the same way to people who work within it.

A lawyer who had complained to a friend about the shockingly unethical behavior of another, very influential lawyer refused to tell the bar association what he knew when it was considering a charge of unethical behavior brought by a client against the influential lawyer. The first lawyer had been the target of intimidating threats from his powerful colleague and knew that if he made trouble, those threats would be carried out. He also knew that this man's friends in high positions within the bar association would not want to see their crony disciplined.

So many people in the system—like the consumers they are supposed to serve—feel overwhelmed by it and by the "experts" and the powerful above them. And they—like the consumer— may hate it, too. The following description applies to a very broad set of situations today and is becoming increasingly prevalent:

From a feminist perspective, Jennifer Dale and Peggy Foster see the limited aid extended by social workers as reinforcing inequalities: "By acting as the rationers of scarce resources welfare professionals provide a useful buffer between women's demands and a State which will not meet those demands. Welfare professionals, rationing resources on a personal and individual basis, help to disguise the collective nature of women's oppression." Knowing that as a professional helper you aren't really going to be helping clients get on their feet produces a sense of demoralization—primarily among clients but also among social workers. After all their training, social workers discover that while their agencies do provide some help to clients, at best they can barely scratch the surface of the problem. Within agencies, tensions can build and explode.[14]

One reason some authorities feel daunted by the system in which they work is frustration or guilt about not having more power and resources than they actually have.

> When I headed a women's center, many of the women had genuine, legitimate, pressing needs—for space, funding, information, or moral support. Although I would dearly have loved to have met all those needs or arranged to have them met, the center was underfunded, understaffed, and already overcrowded. From the point of view of some of the women who came to the center seeking help, I appeared unwilling to help, because they were unaware of how few resources I could put my hands on and how many requests were being made for those resources.

—As the Nuremberg trials dramatically demonstrated, *many people base their behavior on doing what they are ordered to do.* There are a host of reasons why different individuals follow orders, and whole books have been written about the subject. Many of the reasons are discussed in this chapter, such as needing the job for financial reasons, needing to feel supported by the system, and so on. But I give an example here from my own experience of being pressured to follow orders, because it illustrated vividly for me at the time how tempting it can be to obey orders so as to avoid trouble in the workplace.

> I was a single parent contributing heavily to the support of my two children, who lived with me. I constantly felt exhausted from full-time work at a clinic and raising my children alone. The last thing I needed was a further drain on my emotional energy. I tried to do my job well, both for my patients' sakes and to avoid hassle from my supervisors. One day, I phoned a psychiatrist who had previously seen a patient of mine and diagnosed her as "psychotically depressed." The psychiatrist was out when I called, so I asked that he phone me back. When he did, I asked him what psychotic behavior he had seen in the woman. Having only recently received my Ph.D., I believed that I was so unskilled that I had missed her psychotic signs, and this alarmed me. The psychiatrist was silent for a moment and then replied, "Well, uh, she had had a hysterectomy, but I didn't think she should have been *that* depressed." At that point, I realized that the woman had not indeed been psychotic. The psychiatrist

called the clinic director to complain on two grounds: I had backed him into a corner, "grilling" him about the psychosis, and I had left word with his secretary to call "Dr. Caplan," without indicating that I was "only" a psychologist, not a psychiatrist like him. When my supervisor spoke to me about this incident, he told me that in such a situation, the next time, my role should be to sense that the psychiatrist had a weak ego and "work to build it up." I did not believe that it was my responsibility to build up a psychiatrist's weak ego, but my supervisor had a great deal of control over how difficult or easy my life at the clinic would be, and I felt intensely the pressure to follow his orders.

—Some authorities use such disempowering techniques as not disclosing all the facts because *they don't want to have to watch the consumer become upset upon hearing unpalatable truths* (such as "I'm afraid we don't know how to help you").[15] Or they may use the technique of not listening to clients because *they find it disconcerting to hear about so much distress*.

My doctor recently seemed not to listen to a question I asked him, and I believe it was because he didn't want to hear me become upset. I had had my first mammogram, and he had told me it was routine, just to get baseline information in case we should need it in the future. A few days after the test, he phoned me at home and said in a gentle voice, "The radiologist saw something that looked suspicious, so we want you to go back for another test, but it's probably nothing." I said I understood that it was probably nothing but wondered what the suspicion was about. My doctor said, "In most of these cases it's really nothing at all." Feeling increasingly agitated, I said, "Yes, I hear you. But when you say it looks 'suspicious,' in cases that don't turn out to be nothing, is it cancer? Is that what we are talking about?" He again said, "It's probably nothing." Ironically, although I think he wished to reassure and calm me, his refusal to give me a straight answer upset me more than if he had just said, "Yes, cancer is only rarely found in these cases, but that is what we worry about."

—*They don't want to be the butt of anger from a consumer who blames them for not providing help and services.*

Resa was on the fast track, aiming to become a manager in the weight-loss clinic where she worked. She worked seventy hours a week, trying to impress her bosses by her industriousness, and she didn't want anything to stand in the way of her goal of being promoted very soon. When a married couple, both of whom had attended the clinic in the hope of losing enough weight to alleviate their problems with diabetes and high blood pressure, complained to her because the weight-loss program had not helped them lose as much weight as Resa had promised, Resa dismissed them curtly, saying she suspected they hadn't really stuck to the diet. She was afraid that their complaint could block her career advancement, and she also simply hated dealing with people's anger.

—*They get caught up in their own system and actually come to believe in its myths and explanations*. "Bad things happen to people who deserve them" is one such myth, and another is "The most powerful people in this system always know best." Over time, they come to believe in their own framework, so when they perpetuate myths, they *think* they are telling the truth. One reason people believe in their institutions' myths is that belief systems do simplify life by limiting the number of options from which we have to choose. But those belief systems often are not created or do not develop to serve consumers.

In a psychological clinic, therapists conducted lengthy assessments of families of delinquent teenagers and then sent detailed recommendations to the courts about what should be done. The recommendations ranged from placement of the youths in reform schools or foster homes, to putting them on probation, to ordering the parents into marital therapy. At a clinic party where joke gifts were presented, one staff member gave another a roulette wheel on which each segment represented a possible recommendation. When the staff saw the wheel, many laughed nervously in recognition of the frequent arbitrariness of their recommendations. Furthermore, they were acutely aware that they almost never followed up to determine whether specific kinds of recommendations had worked in specific situations; thus, no one really knew whether or not their recommendations were valid. But at no time after the party did the clinic staff ever seriously discuss this as a problem. They were too caught up in following the clinic's practices, and these practices included not discussing the extent to which their recommendations were unsupported by research about their effectiveness. Their shared myth was that what they did was helpful; that myth might have been justified, but no one had yet found out.

Such adherence to established practices and belief systems simplifies life for those who work in the system but does not necessarily help their consumers.

—*When someone seeks help or service, their behavior tends to signal submissiveness, and when all else is equal, this tends to elicit dominant behavior from the other person.*[16] Whether or not I realize it, if someone speaks meekly to me, I tend to reply in an authoritative way (and vice versa), and the pervasiveness of this tendency has been well documented. The chances that the other person will behave in a dominant way increase, of course, when one person truly has more power or resources than the other. Dominant behavior may involve the way one sits or stands (the powerful take up more space; the powerless constrict their limbs) or feeling free to use the whole range of disempowering techniques.[17]

—*They need to feel competent and professional.* Carniol reports:

> Students [in social work] are assessed not only on how well they relate to clients but also on how well they respect the agency's mandate (and its limitations) and fit into the agency's work. Assessments of student performance are rooted in those social work theories that value "helping" clients adjust to existing conditions. Not that students are expected to issue directives for clients to follow. The process is far more subtle. Students are encouraged to ask about what clients want, to empathize with their problems, to explain what the agency can or cannot do, and to offer help only on terms acceptable to the particular agency.[18]

—*They've never been in the consumer's shoes.*

Even in the scientifically based world of medicine, knowing how it feels to be a patient is so important that some medical schools are beginning to include a stint in the role of patient for their students. In addition to learning about the emotional aspects of patienthood, doctors report that, by putting themselves in the patient's position, they become more skilled at encouraging patients to talk freely about their current symptoms and their medical histories, essential information for the doctor in making diagnoses and planning treatment. This concept is the basis of the movie *The Doctor*. When a friend of mine was a medical student, he developed a bleeding ulcer and was hospitalized in the medical center where his medical school was based. He reported that this experience had a profound impact on him: "After that, every time I ordered a blood test or a gastroscopy (internal examination of the digestive tract) for a patient, I remembered how it had felt when I had those tests, and that made me think carefully about whether or not the tests were warranted."

—*The need to believe that they will never end up in the consumer's situation.* When we face an ill, troubled, or needy person, it is natural to hope that we will never be in such a state. We need to believe that the world is safe for us. But that is hard to believe without assuming it is safe for others, too. And that need leads easily to victim-blame: People who work in institutions are like observers of accidents, who need to believe that *you* are unemployed or lost *your* child or need a loan because *you* did something wrong. Authorities who can believe that you brought your troubles on yourself can then believe that if *they* behave differently from you, they can avoid such troubles.[19] Examples of this motive span the range of seriousness—from the television repairman who asked me if I (height 5 feet 2 inches, poor upper-body strength) had caused my set to malfunction by throwing it across the room, to the police officer who told a rape victim that *his* daughters would never be raped, because he had taught them to dress modestly.

—*They are overworked, and when their time and energy are limited, it is often easiest to resort to techniques that hurt those they are supposed to help.*[20] Clients/consumers come and go, but one works with one's colleagues every day, and one's supervisors decide on one's pay raises and promotions. These hard facts tend to increase the chances of authorities treating consumers in either an aggressive or a cavalier manner.

In the field of social work, for instance, the worker's practice is supposed to be based on such values as the dignity of the client and making sure the client "no longer feels entirely alone with the problem." But, Ben Carniol points out, "When caseloads number well over 160 individuals and families, it becomes impossible for the worker to know clients except on a superficial level":

> From a service point of view, I don't even have time to listen to clients. In one recent month my total caseload was over 215 cases! I burnt out last August. During one hour then I had as many as five cases of evictions to deal with. It got to the point that emotionally I gave as little as I could to each client. Of course clients realize it and get resentful.[21]

And a frustrated but perceptive patient in a hospital says,

> Nurses are overwhelmed with work. . . . There are not enough nurses. They don't want to do anything. They need more discipline. Doctors have a broader outlook and aren't so petty. . . . But then nurses are harassed by both the patients and the system, aren't they?[22]

When those at the top, for whatever reasons, impose impossible quantities of work on their subordinates, then the front-line workers often take it out on the clients/consumers, either through aggressive or dismissive behavior or through slapdash jobs.

—*Some people use disempowering techniques because that is what they have to do to keep their jobs, and they need their jobs.* They need financial security. The job may be their only source of financial support for themselves, their partners, their children, or their elderly parents. They may have large debts. Even after leaving one job, publicly disagreeing with a former employer could jeopardize a current position.

> In an article about the U.S. Department of Justice shredding potentially incriminating documents at the end of the Bush presidency, a former Department of Justice official asked the interviewer not to give his name as a source of the information: "|'It embarrasses me that I don't have the courage to go on the

record,' he said, 'but I still have a family to support and I know the power of the DOJ and the ruthlessness with which it is now being exercised.'."[23]

And the first woman, Black, Jew, person with a disability, lesbian, or gay person in that office or institution may feel intense pressure to follow the rules in order both to keep their job and to avoid messing up the chances for other members of their group to be hired.

Just as a leg can be broken in a car accident, a fall, or a barroom brawl, so can any disempowering technique come from authorities whose motives span the whole range of possibilities. Just as therapists point out that the particular *cause* of an emotional problem rarely determines the *nature of the symptoms* a patient will develop, so a single motive can lead authorities to use a variety of techniques, and a single technique can be used by authorities with a wide variety of motives. For instance, when I started work at a psychological clinic, I was mystified by the alphabet soup I encountered. A colleague told me that my new patient "lived in an OHC building and had both a PO and a CAS worker"—code for "the patient lives in subsidized housing and had a probation officer and a worker from the child welfare agency." As I learned what the initials signified, I realized that I was more inclined to take the time to explain their meanings to students I supervised if I liked the students personally than if I did not. But also, the longer I worked there, the more I tended to forget what new people needed to be taught about the abbreviations. Even my own motives for using jargon or technical language have ranged from using my power as license to cause a bit of discomfort in someone less powerful to a need to use shortcuts and a consequent insensitivity to the needs of others due to my heavy workload.

Surveying the variety of ways that authorities behave, Steinem writes, "Long-term hierarchies have produced a few people at the top who use power poorly, a lot of people in the middle who wait for orders and approval, and many more at the bottom who feel powerless and resentful."[24] But people with a broad range of motives can use even the most blatant techniques. Consider, for instance, the technique of intimidation. A friend from my college days visited my city after he became the publisher of a large city newspaper. Over dinner, he told me that he had learned he has to be very careful when he makes suggestions to his employees about how the newspaper could be improved. He said, "I try to offer negative feedback or suggestions as gently and supportively as possible, because I have found out that people who have less power than I do regard me as extremely powerful, so that everything I say has a far greater impact than I intend it to have. What I might consider a mild suggestion tends to be taken very hard by some of my employees." In contrast, the superintendent of a city school system told me how glad he is to have so much power, because "What I say, goes. When I tell my staff to jump, they jump—and I *like* it!" Apparently, both the publisher and the superintendent were intimidating to members of their staffs, but their intentions and motives were clearly quite different.

Most of the motives discussed in this chapter involve emotional factors—primarily fears and needs—that lead authorities to treat consumers in ways that make us feel stupid and powerless. Interacting with many of these motives is the pressure on authorities to avoid questioning how their system works. That pressure, as well as forces that keep consumers from thinking critically about systems and authorities, are addressed in the next chapter.

5

Asking Questions

Why It's Done So Rarely

To see deep into the structure of one tyranny is to understand something basic about all forms of oppression. It is totalitarian. Like other authoritarian systems, it requires a suspension and suppression of critical questioning. . . .

—Jeffrey Moussaieff Masson[1]

The primary aim of this book is to urge consumers to ask more questions, most importantly, "Is it really all my fault that I didn't get the help I sought?" From that one question follow many others, all directed toward trying to understand why you didn't get that help, and this means doing some careful and critical thinking. A related aim is to urge authorities to think critically about what they do and why.

This chapter and the next two are about the reasons why consumers and authorities do so little critical thinking. This chapter is about some general reasons for the lack of such thinking, and Chapter 6 is a kind of behind-the-scenes look at the obstacles to such thinking by those in positions of authority. Chapter 7 is focussed on the forces that discourage consumers from thinking critically about the way they are treated, and it also includes some specific critical thinking steps that consumers can begin to take. I am always dismayed to hear people assert that they don't know how to think critically or that they don't like to question authorities because they don't know where to begin. I find this distressing because most critical thinking involves simple logic or common sense. If you went for a walk one day and saw a dog "fall" *up*, you would immediately wonder what force had been strong enough to oppose the downward pull of gravity. If your child wants to swallow a wild mushroom when you are in the countryside, you first find out whether it is poisonous, and you check to make sure that there are no animal droppings on it. *There is no important difference* between this kind of questioning attitude and critical thinking about what authorities and experts say and do. What is different, of course, is the risk involved and the power issues when we as consumers question authorities or when we authorities question other authorities. These matters are discussed in detail in this chapter and Chapters 6 and 7.

In principle, a curious, questioning attitude is considered admirable in our culture. Many parents boast about their children's insistence on knowing the why and the how about every detail of the workings of the world. But adults, whether as authorities or consumers, too rarely think critically about what we are doing or what is being done to us. I mean "critical" not in the sense of "negative" but rather in the sense of asking questions about what we are told and how we are treated rather than immediately accepting it. But many people find it disconcerting or even scary to think critically, even when it is *not* just negative. I've taught critical thinking in my courses for close to twenty-five years, and I am continually surprised by how uncomfortable some students become when I urge them to think logically and questioningly. One graduate student approached me after the second meeting of one of my courses and said, with her chin quivering and her eyes filled with tears, "I have to drop this course, because it's interesting to delve into claims I've heard all my life and accepted as true—like 'men are more assertive than women'—but I'm frightened to think that there may be no real, absolute truth, nothing I can count on for sure. Once I start questioning what I've always believed, what if it turns out that there's nothing left?"

I told her that my feeling is that it's better to find out when our beliefs and assumptions are wrong than to base our attitudes and actions on unjustified or unproven claims. Yes, I said, that can make us uncomfortable, because we have less certainty in our lives than before, but a *sense* of certainty based on untruths surely isn't healthy or helpful in the long run. So deeply ingrained was this student's fear of questioning authority, however, that she did indeed drop the course. For some people, questioning authority is frightening because it feels too much like questioning the word of God, something they have been forbidden to do since childhood.

The other, more encouraging type of reaction I have had from students and general audiences at my lectures has been their sense of great freedom and exhilaration when they are encouraged to stop being passive consumers of authorities' claims. I have used this approach in public lectures and in graduate and undergraduate courses and even in working with children. Despite a third-grade teacher's warning that "children of that age simply cannot think abstractly enough to do critical thinking," Margaret Secord-Gilbert and I developed an efficient way to encourage primary-school children to think critically: We have them design their own easy-to-manage research studies (e.g., "Are boys ruder than girls?") and then practice finding the problems and inadequacies in their own research.[2] My son, Jeremy B. Caplan, and I have written a book applying critical thinking principles to research on sex differences for high school and college students.[3] In all these projects, we have discovered that no secret techniques are required to think critically, only a willingness to ask questions and to think logically. And people of all ages who are, even briefly, encouraged to think in this way often tell us that that encouragement has changed their lives: They now feel less like inadequately educated captives of the claims that experts make and more like active, curious consumers of information. Just as they try to find out, before buying, whether a new breakfast cereal is as nourishing as its marketers claim, they now want to know whether headlines such as "Boys better at math due to male hormones" are based not just on research but on responsible, careful research before deciding whether or not to believe them. Most people are surprised to discover how little research supports some common beliefs. Failing to question such claims as "Teenagers' rebelliousness is inevitable and healthy" has enormous impact on the emotional and interpersonal areas of our lives, and failing to question such claims as "Chemotherapy cures cancer" can be a matter of life and death.

This chapter is about why we need critical thinking and what keeps so many of us—authorities and consumers—from doing it. As in earlier chapters, many of the examples here come from either the medical realm because few of us escape its impact, and many are from my own areas of research on psychological sex differences and psychology of women, because I am most directly familiar with such examples and most people can immediately relate to them.

CRITICAL THINKING: WHY WE NEED IT

The *need* for critical thinking comes into sharp relief when the experts contradict each other: As Alexander Pope wrote, "Who shall decide when doctors disagree?"[4] A close family member of mine, while hospitalized recently for a digestive tract problem, experienced a brief heartbeat irregularity. One of his doctors told him matter-of-factly, "Oh, that's a side effect of the medication I prescribed for you. I'll lower the dosage. Nothing to worry about. Nothing at all." Another doctor said, "No, it couldn't possibly have been the medication. We should probably put you on long-term heart medication right away and keep you here under observation for several days." In such a situation, a patient who hesitates to question doctors not only will feel intensely anxious over these conflicting claims but might well worry that decisions about his care will be based more on which doctor has more power in the hospital chain of command than on sound medical reasoning. And that could certainly cause one's blood pressure to rise or one's heart to beat irregularly.

In less life-threatening but certainly anxiety-provoking circumstances, parents—especially mothers—often despair of knowing how to raise children because of the dramatically contradictory advice from experts.[5] One parenting expert will advise, "Be sure to include all of the children in family councils when decisions are made, because it's important for them to feel included." Another will say, "Parents should make decisions for the family and *not* include children in that process, because it makes children uncomfortable when adults don't make it clear who has the power in the family and who makes the rules." How are we to know whom to believe, especially when each speaks with great certainty? No mega-expert will tell us *when* we should try each kind of approach. And as I have written elsewhere, rarely does either of these experts warn us that no single approach works all the time. So if we try one and it fails, we tend to think it is our fault for not carrying it out well enough.[6]

The need for critical thinking is also clear when we consider the consequences of authorities' sloppy or biased thinking. A woman I'll call Ms. Field nearly lost her home and her car on account of the sloppy thinking or laziness of the personnel director in the company where she worked. Ms. Field became ill and had to go on sick leave. Because recovery from her serious illness was extremely slow, and she knew her sick leave was about to run out, she applied for long-term disability. Her employer had just switched insurance companies, and she was told to send the long-term disability application to their original company because it had been the insurer when she first took sick. After many weeks, that insurer rejected her claim (perhaps they were angry about having lost her employer's account). Ms. Field asked her personnel director what to do next, and he replied that she would have to return to work (against doctors' orders) or take time off without pay. The new insurer refused to consider her long-term disability claim, he said, because when she fell ill they were not her insurer. Worried because family responsibilities had drained her savings, so that unpaid time off work would mean losing her house and car, Ms. Field did some research and learned that she was eligible for a second period of sick leave. When she asked the personnel director why he hadn't informed her of that option, he replied, "Because you can't have two sick leaves for the same illness." (In addition to careless thinking, the personnel director might also have been motivated by the wish to keep his company's insurance premiums down, of course.) Had the director put his mind to it, he probably could have come up with the helpful idea Ms. Field later had in conversation with a friend. The friend observed that fighting the uncaring bureaucracy and facing the prospect of having no home or car had made Ms. Field severely anxious and depressed, to the point where she couldn't even do a bit of writing for work as she lay in bed. This gave them the idea of having a therapist document her emotional problems and then requesting a second sick leave due to emotional disturbance.

In a quite different example of careless thinking, eighty-nine-year-old woman died recently of AIDS, but she wasn't diagnosed as suffering from AIDS until shortly before her death, even though on admission to the hospital she was suffering from three common signs of AIDS: a particular type of pneumonia, dementia, and malnutrition.[7] Most of the doctors didn't dream she might have AIDS, for two reasons: (1) Older people frequently have the above problems but do not have AIDS (although they rarely have all three simultaneously), and (2) because this patient was eighty-nine years old, the doctors asked her only whether she had had a blood transfusion or was an intravenous drug user, and neither was true of her. Although those are two ways to get AIDS, sexual contact with someone who is HIV-positive is another; but because she was old, medical staff failed to ask her about sexual activity. When the patient's face later broke out in the kinds of purple marks typical of AIDS-related Kaposi's sarcoma, the staff asked further questions and learned that her husband had been addicted to drugs he took intravenously, and the patient and her husband

had had sex until his death five years earlier. It has been documented that the symptoms of AIDS may not appear until as
long as seven years after exposure to the HIV virus. Some people might jump to the defense of these doctors on the grounds
that cases of AIDS in eighty-nine-year-old women are rare, but
do we really want to rewrite physicians' job descriptions to
read "Diagnosing obvious and fairly obvious illnesses"?

Another instance of biased and sloppy thinking in the health
field is reported by physician Jean Hamilton.[8] Even after toxic
shock syndrome was recognized as a potentially fatal illness
associated with the use of tampons, she writes, it took the Food
and Drug Administration seven years to begin *deliberations*
about labeling tampons' content. Health officials were even
slower to regulate sperm banks than blood transfusions as
sources of AIDS. Hamilton believes that, because blood transfusions can transmit infection to people of either sex but tampons and donated sperm only to women, these examples
illustrate the ways biases—in this case, leading to neglect of
women's health—can dramatically shape health policy. Hamilton suggests that "the problem was two-fold: first at the level of
failing to integrate and appreciate the meaning of existing
information; and second, at the level of failing to act appropri-
ately, in a prompt and timely manner."[9]

Similarly, health and social problems affecting primarily less
powerful or wealthy people—such as sickle-cell anemia for
Blacks or homelessness for the poor—tend to receive little
research money or government policymakers' attention unless
and until (as with gays and AIDS) significant lobbying, political
action, and media attention are developed by or for the affected
group—or when it begins to have an impact on the dominant
group. Scientific reasoning and humane attitudes are not
applied with an even hand to all problems, and as a result,
those who have problems associated more with low-status than
high-status people are those most likely to suffer or die.

When the field is not hard science, the lack of careful work
and thinking can also have far-reaching consequences. The theory that immediate and total emotional "bonding" between
parent (especially mother) and child is essential to the child's

healthy development has made countless mothers and fathers feel guilty for not experiencing that immediate and total connection before leaving the delivery room, and many mothers have feared they would destroy their children psychologically if they were not full-time mothers. Adoptive parents and parents whose premature children spent their first weeks of life in incubators have despaired of having normal relationships with their children because of missing the chance to bond in the infants' first days. Fortunately, researchers such as Beverly Birns[10] and Stella Chess and Alexander Thomas[11] provide ample evidence that immediate, total bonding is not essential for children's emotional health—but their work is known to only a fraction of parents who have been told that the most extreme form of bonding theory is the truth.

The rarity of critical thinking in regard to knowledge can have great impact even outside the sciences per se because science can affect other fields. For instance, although scientists' primary preoccupation is supposed to be knowledge, judges are supposed to focus on justice. To mete out justice, judges are supposed to be wise and able to go beyond personal biases in making decisions. Hordes of citizens turn to the judicial-legal system, seeking fair judgments, only to find that the system is often unjust and that many judges base their decisions not on rational, logical thinking about principles of law, not on humane principles, but on their own intense, personal prejudices. Ironically, they may believe that these prejudices are truths, because they have learned (or been supported in) them from so-called scientists. For example, the media have been filled with stories of judges who imposed only minimal sentences on adult men who raped preschool or primary-school girls, on the theory that the young children were seductive or promiscuous. This theory is regularly presented by psychoanalysts as indisputable truth, even though its author, Sigmund Freud, lied about his data to justify the theory.[12] And recently, a powerful judge who was asked to rule on some native people's rights to a large area of land threw out the aboriginals' claim, saying in his decision that they are primitive people and that their ancestors were "nasty, brutish and short."[13] The classification of nonwhite people as "primitive" has been a racist activity of many influential anthropologists, so it is encouraging that some contemporary anthropologists are vociferously objecting to this judge's labeling of native people.[14]

Going one step beyond careless and biased thinking, we encounter outright cheating and falsification by authorities (as mentioned briefly in Chapter 3). No less an expert than a former deputy inspector of weights and measures says he

> could write a book about cheating and chiselling by merchants. The unsuspecting customer assumes that because scales are automatic and electronic, the printout is accurate. This is not true. Scales are mechanical devices that can and do go out of adjustment. An unscrupulous merchant can fix a scale so it will short the customer. . . . It was my job to see that every weighing and measuring device in the city was inspected and tested. We visited every gas station, factory, grocery store, bakery, butcher shop, rail yard, junkyard, foundry, steel mill and department store. . . . Gasoline pumps may also be tampered with and rigged.[15]

All these reasons, then—authorities' contradictory pronouncements, their sloppy and prejudiced thinking, and their active distortion of truth—constitute compelling proof of the need for us all to do more critical thinking.

WHY EXPERTS AND CONSUMERS VOICE SO LITTLE DOUBT

Armed with all the jargon, status, and money at their command, making confident claims about what is the truth, *experts can be very convincing to their colleagues and the public.* I was disturbed but, in a sense, impressed by the earnest nods of agreement from a roomful of psychiatrists as one of their number said in a presentation, "I knew that this woman patient was making no progress in her therapy with me, because she refused to acknowledge having any sexual fantasies about me whatsoever." These men shared a particular belief about what indicates progress in therapy, and not one uttered a peep of doubt. It is not surprising that many laypeople, knowing themselves to be uninformed about the details of theories and ignorant of the jargon, would also be reluctant to disagree. A professional's colleagues may be silenced by fear of ostracism for questioning accepted doctrine, and laypeople may be silenced from fear of being unable to make a good case to support their criticisms or simply feel that they would seem stupid if they spoke up.

There are so many reasons we don't voice our doubts or questions. We'll look first at forces that silence both experts and consumers, then at some that specifically affect experts, and finally at some that particularly affect consumers.

One factor that can affect any of us begins to operate when we are very young, if our curious queries about why the sky is blue, why things fall down instead of up, and how the earth revolves around the sun exhaust our parents to the point that they begin to bristle or get angry. *We don't want to upset our parents, and so we reduce the number of questions we ask or even stop asking altogether.* I'm quite sure that my relative comfort with critical thinking began because my parents and my Uncle Billy were so encouraging when, as a child, I asked questions. As I later learned from many years as a single parent, such unstinting encouragement is hard to sustain. However, even overworked parents can make it clear to children that we may not have time to answer all their questions but that it is good that they are asking.

Although in theory, children learn to ask and explore in school, teachers often feel pressured by the needs of the thirty-odd children in the class, as well as their school board's requirements that they teach certain facts and information by specified deadlines (and there *is* so much information that probably should be taught) and train students to score well on standardized tests to make the school look good or to get into college. As a result, *teachers may not find or make the time to encourage children to do critical thinking.* Furthermore, most teachers have not been taught critical skills themselves and so they do not see a need to critique the material they are presenting. In fact, students are often not much encouraged to ask questions at all. An experience I had in high school stands out because it was so unusual. In most of my classes, I was quick to ask for explanations when I didn't understand what the teacher was saying. In a high school physics course, I was one of only two girls, and whenever I raised my hand to ask a question, some of the boys would gesture to me to put it down. Sometimes, they would whisper, "Don't waste class time, Caplan!" One day the instructor, Dr. "Heavy" Henderson (a kind, slim man who had acquired the nickname when he played football) noticed what they were doing and snapped at them, "Don't you *dare* try to stop her from asking questions! At least *she* asks when she doesn't understand something."

Even today, there is evidence that girls are more likely than boys to be discouraged from thinking critically: A recent, large-scale study revealed that teachers call on girls for answers less frequently and reward them "more often for compliance than for critical thinking."[16] Small wonder, then, that women more than men feel reluctant and incapable of questioning what authorities tell them. And because impulses toward doing critical thinking are likely to be squelched by criticism, it is significant that, in general, teachers have been shown to interact more positively with Anglo- than with Mexican-American students and to criticize the latter more often.[17]

Even intelligent, white male students can be the target of anger for asking questions, and it is particularly distressing when the anger comes from a teacher. When Ed was in high school, he was interested in learning some math formulas and when to use them. However, Ed also wanted to know *why* each formula was used in a particular situation. Unaware that the teacher usually taught science and knew little about math, he asked the teacher several questions. Much later, Ed's parents figured out that the teacher must have been embarrassed not to know the answers to Ed's questions, but instead of simply admitting that or offering to help him find out, he became enraged, grabbed Ed by the shirt front, yanked his head down on his desk, and held it there. Although this is an extreme example, the sad fact is that many teachers, like many authorities in any field, operate on the assumption that they are supposed to know everything about their subjects. I find that poignant, because when I became a teacher, as soon as I realized that I could *not* know everything, I started telling students that and felt quite relieved and free. Even better, so did the students, because they knew that if I didn't pretend to know it all myself, then I certainly wouldn't consider them foolish for asking questions or not understanding all the material.

The parents and teachers who don't make children's critical thinking a priority are acting in accordance with *a whole culture in which critical thinking is discouraged.* A pair of beliefs underlies all this reluctance to think critically and to question. Those beliefs are that

1. Science produces truth.
2. Powerful people do what is right.

It's important to notice that these two beliefs are based on an all-or-nothing view of life: Any given thing is true or false, correct or incorrect, moral or immoral, polite or rude. As a way of calling attention to how misguided it is, this view has been named "dichotomania,"[18] a frenetic insistence on either-or ways of classifying information and experience. As a researcher, I constantly see that what was once considered true is later shown to be partly or completely false. But if, when we hear a claim, we feel pressed to classify it as simply true or simply false, then our freedom to assess the evidence honestly will be severely restricted.

Feeling this pressure once led me into a mortifying situation from which I learned an invaluable lesson. Before conducting the research for my dissertation, I made predictions about how the results would turn out. But when I gathered my data, the results turned out somewhat differently. It was frequently rumored that one couldn't get one's degree if one's predictions were wrong. Nevertheless, I believed I described my results and drew my conclusions honestly when I wrote the dissertation. During the oral examination about my dissertation, however, a professor turned to the final sentence I had written, read it aloud, and asked me to comment. To my shame, in the

words I heard him read I was claiming that my results supported my predictions.

Seeing how pressures within my milieu had affected me
taught me a lesson I've never forgotten. I remembered feeling
determined, as I wrote, to restrict my claims to what I truly
had found. I had talked with friends about my fear of failing to
obtain the degree because my predictions had not been borne
out, and I was certain I had overcome my fear. Knowing that I
distorted my conclusion—despite my conscious intentions—
when I felt my Ph.D. was at stake, I can easily believe that
researchers distort the truth when million-dollar grants, promotions, or professional reputations are at stake. Naturally, I
rewrote my conclusion, but had I felt comfortable in the first
place writing that I *seemed* to have found *partial* evidence for
some of my predictions, I might not have distorted my conclusion in the first place. In such ways does the pressure to see the
world in all-or-nothing terms discourage us from critical, clear
thinking.

Another major impediment to critical thinking is the fact
that science and technology have produced some significant
achievements—miracles, some would say, and so *both experts
and the public tend to assume there is a cure or solution for
everything.* Whether we are scientists or laypeople, knowing,
for instance, that antibiotics can rapidly cure some infections
that used to be fatal makes us long to believe that anything can
be cured. This belief puts pressure on the expert always to *be*
the curer or problem solver, and some experts deal with such
pressure by becoming defensive and angry in the face of questioning. The belief in experts' powers to cure and solve gives
scientists and technologists an intimidating, awe-inspiring aura
that can make it hard for consumers to question what they do.
And because the language of science and technology is so often
hard to understand, consumers are silenced by the fear of
seeming foolish or of voicing concerns that are *truly* nonsensi-
cal to those in the know.

There is a parallel here with the message of the movie *Field
of Dreams*, in which the hero hears a voice telling him, "If you

build it [a baseball field], they will come." *If you call it Science and Truth, the people will believe it.* The power of such naming is truly astonishing. For example, as Jeri Wine has remarked, until recently approximately 70 percent of all the people studied in psychological experiments were boys and men, yet from all-male studies conclusions were drawn about the "true" nature of human behavior.[19] Lawrence Kohlberg studied only a small group of (probably all-white) men but claimed he had discovered that people develop morally, going to higher stages as they grow up, and that the average male reaches a higher stage than the average female.[20] Many years after this research became widely believed, Carol Gilligan drew attention to his all-male sample and pointed out how bad either sex would look if the other sex were used as the standard of normality.[21] But until Gilligan's work was published, Kohlberg's work was generally assumed to be true.

We also tend to accept unthinkingly what authorities tell us because we *need* to believe that the people whom we ask for help actually *can* help us. As Kramer has written in regard to physicians, "we seem to need sworn enemies of death. They will disappoint us, sooner or later, in every case, but we have allowed them to take on power and privilege, and prejudice, in return, perhaps, for both their practical and their ceremonial chores."[22] At least when it comes to doctors, our need to believe they can do anything was fed by some medical achievements that seemed truly miraculous:

> "After the Second World War, when things like penicillin came along, people began to believe that anything they had wrong with them, the physician could quickly diagnose and fix," says Dr. Bruce Squires, head of publications for the Canadian Medical Association in Ottawa.
>
> "Physicians, while they knew it wasn't true, began to believe their own reputation," he says.
>
> "But it became evident this doesn't work. Physicians can't cure everything."[23]

Like science and technology, some government initiatives have had positive consequences. People who lived through the

Depression in the United States saw the great achievements of the Works Progress Administration in putting people back to work, for instance—and *it is tempting to believe that governments and government agencies can solve a host of problems.* Furthermore, it is well known that government bodies often have information that is not available to anyone else, so, as with science and technology, those who seek help from them are often silenced by their fear of making objections that will expose oppose them to ridicule. For instance, American Gulf War soldiers now suffering from bizarre, chronic physical problems have sometimes recently been the target of scathing, dismissive replies from government employees who unjustifiably claim that this couldn't possibly be related to the war. Clients may be unaware that, if they are uninformed, it is because information has been purposely or unintentionally withheld from them.

Medical and physical science research is generally thought to be freer from bias and distortion than any other research fields. We are likely to be more surprised by news that a cancer researcher funded by a major government body has faked his data (as happened not long ago) than that a psychologist has faked data about, say, competitiveness. We wrongly assume that, because the stakes of medical research can be life or death, medical scientists will avoid sloppy thinking and research and wouldn't dream of distorting or faking their results. Most people's image of chemists and physicists is of men characterized by total objectivity, interest in truth, and complete dedication to their work. Thus, we tend to feel, there is no need for us nonspecialists to think critically about scientists' claims.

There is, however, great cause to do such thinking. The compelling movie *Lorenzo's Oil* is the true story of nonscientists Michaela and Augusto Odone's discovery of a cure for a rare genetic defect that was killing their son, after medical researchers insisted against all reason that their son remain on a treatment that was making him worse. As Gordon notes, "The powerful technology and very real achievements of biomedicine have encouraged many physicians to regard themselves as scientists carefully sifting experimental evidence and bringing highly rationalized therapeutic procedures to bear on carefully diagnosed disease entities." However, Gordon explains, research sponsored by the U.S. House of Representatives "suggests that a large percentage of diagnostic procedures are improperly done or interpreted [Brook, 1973]," and a study from the Congressional Office of Technology Assessment "indicates that only '10 to 20 percent of all procedures currently used in medical practice' have been justified by controlled studies."[24]

When the Food and Drug Administration's Alan Lisook analyzed investigations conducted by his agency during the previous ten years, he "found that nearly 200 studies contained so many flaws that the ability of the tested drugs to produce the claimed results was seriously questioned. About 40 studies exhibited recklessness or outright fraud."[25] In one example, a "promising young heart specialist" published made-up data: "In a six-year period, Slutsky churned out 161 research papers and at one time he completed one every 10 days. Even by today's pressurized standards, two articles a year is considered prolific."[26]

Fear of punishment for threatening the powers-that-be is a powerful obstacle to thinking critically, both for laypeople and for people who work within oppressive systems but are not at the top of their hierarchies. We may believe we are asking the simplest, most innocent question, but those in positions of power may know—or fear—that an honest answer to that question would expose the flaws in them or their system. Thus, they may fear that we are trying to destroy them or their system. In *Lorenzo's Oil*, the parents of the seriously ill boy ask the doctor why he insists that they keep their son on a special diet, because in the six weeks on the diet he has gotten worse. As the movie clearly shows, in doing conventional research, *scientists feel compelled to complete their projects as originally planned, regardless of the effects on the people who are their guinea pigs.* Indeed, there is the real danger that funding agencies will demand that their money be returned if the proposed study is not completed. Lorenzo's doctor, then, felt trapped when

Lorenzo's parents asked their question. He had to choose between ruining his research (he risked losing his funding and hurting his professional reputation for not completing the work) and hurting the children who were the subjects of the research.

In order to discourage their colleagues, their subordinates, and laypeople from asking questions, *authorities sometimes use such techniques as labeling* (calling us impolite, troublemaking, unfeminine if we are women, combative and belligerent if we are men) *or behaving in menacing ways*, ranging from implying that they will stop helping us (or will see that no one in their system helps us) to adopting threatening physical positions. These techniques can certainly make us feel stupid and powerless, the latter especially when we fear losing the help or care that brought us to the authority in the first place.

Critical thinking certainly interferes with routine operations. Therefore, it is realistically associated with resistance or disruption—or even revolution—and that can be scary for people who stand to lose their power and authority. Those who want to avoid change in their system or their personal power find that scary and react by damning the disrupter in a host of ways, hoping to halt the disruption. They call patients "obsessive" if they insist on knowing the possible side effects before accepting a doctor's order to take a drug, they accuse Blacks who want a fair chance at employment of "wanting us to lower our standards," and until recently they have often said that people who ask presidents to justify military action are "unpatriotic Communists." Indeed, the function of intimidation tactics becomes clear as we consider *when* they tend to be used. For instance, owing to powerful medical lobbies, for decades, Americans who wanted socialized medicine were often called Communists; lately, however, that has changed, both as the Soviet Union disintegrated and as it became obvious to more people that the current healthcare system threatens to bankrupt us. Thus, tactics of intimidation are most likely to be used when those who are asking the critical questions are in a minority, and the labels that are used are those most likely to frighten and silence the questioners.

Still another factor that limits critical thinking is *the fear of appearing stupid*. As I've said, having been a curious child, I often found myself asking teachers to explain material I had not understood. Invariably, other students would tell me after class how glad they were that I had asked, because they had also felt confused. "Well, why didn't *you* ask?" I would inquire, and the usual answer was, "I thought there was something wrong with me for not understanding, so I thought I'd look stupid if I asked." This fear of seeming stupid—and even simply different for being the only one to ask—is very strong in most people from early childhood, and few outgrow it completely. Naturally, it interferes with the inclinations of both laypeople and experts to ask questions.

These, then, are some of the factors that tend to squelch the inquisitive impulses of us all. In the next chapter, we look at some factors that specifically limit authorities' inclinations to think critically.

6

What Limits Experts' Critical Thinking?

Not all authorities or experts uncritically swallow dogma or acquiesce to orders and procedures that could hurt the people they are supposed to serve. Most of this chapter is about what tends to prevent authorities from thinking critically, but I want first to describe one of the most fascinating and revealing scenes of a professional going out on a limb to apply his thinking skills—and with a delightful, inspiring outcome.

When I was a graduate student in psychology, many other psychology students were recruited to be cotherapists in a group designed to teach male war veterans clothed in gray hospital garments how to identify and express a wide range of feelings. Most of the veterans were depressed, angry, or very passive, but one I'll call Andy stood out because of his strikingly bizarre behavior. Andy was a young, dashingly handsome Black who had been diagnosed as schizophrenic. The procedures for the group involved having people take turns "directing" scenes in which others practiced naming and expressing their feelings. After each scene, the director was supposed to give feedback to the actor along the lines of, "You expressed your sad feeling very clearly, but I wasn't sure what you thought had caused that feeling." Although some people believe that therapists are comfortable working with all kinds of patients, most of us are not; and when most of us had to work with Andy, we felt pretty hopeless, because he behaved so strangely that he hardly knew where to begin with the feedback. The other men had various degrees of skill at expressing their feelings and identifying what cause them, but Andy regularly sat bolt upright in his chair, staring with glazed eyes as though he saw beyond the rest of us. Often, he seemed unaware that anyone else was even there.

Having been trained to follow the rules of our group's procedures, most of us fumblingly said things to Andy like, "I really wasn't sure which feeling you were trying to express," but we felt hopeless because Andy seemed to be light-years away from being able to express his feelings. In any case, which particular emotion he was having didn't seem important, because he appeared to be in another world altogether. However, all of us except one senior student, Charles, doggedly and unquestioningly followed the procedures we had been given.

One day, when Charles and I were in a three-person group with Andy, it was Charles's turn to be the director, Andy's turn to act out an expressive scene, and my turn to be the actor who was to listen to Andy's expressions. It felt strange to listen attentively to this poor, spaced-out fellow, but I tried to play my part and follow the rules. It seemed rude and unprofessional to think of doing otherwise, but what we were doing seemed to be all for a hopelessly lost cause. Then it was time for Charles to give his feedback to Andy. "Andy," he said matter-of-factly, "when you did your scene, you sat up so straight that you looked extremely uncomfortable, and you stared right through Paula, with your eyes glazed over, so that you didn't even seem to see that she was there!" I was embarrassed for Andy and wondered why Charles had said what he did. Hadn't we been taught that schizophrenics were deeply disturbed, so wasn't it pointless to draw attention to something that Andy was too crazy to be able to control? But Andy immediately relaxed his body, looked straight at Charles, and said, "I do that? No kidding?!" Never have I witnessed such a transformation.

A few weeks later, I got on an elevator, saw a young man dressed spiffily in a sportcoat and tie, and thought, "What an attractive-looking businessman." Then I realized it was Andy. I greeted him and asked him how he was doing, and he replied that he had been out applying for jobs. None of us had ever suspected that he would get that far.

Now, I realize that not every story of a person diagnosed as schizophrenic has such a happy ending. But if all of us therapists had proceeded unthinkingly to deal with Andy in the ways we had been trained to do, he might never have had a chance. And the rest of this chapter is about the many forces that tend to inhibit authorities' questioning attitudes and behavior.

As you read this chapter, keep in mind that virtually every factor that can limit authorities' critical thinking operates in virtually every system and field.

- *They believe they learned the Truth from those who trained them, and their trainers did not encourage them to think critically.*

When I taught courses in psychological testing for many years, my classes included people who had been working for long periods of time as special education teachers. One of my usual exercises was to ask students to administer to each other the tests they would later use on the children. Then I had them list in great detail every factor they could think of—emotional, cognitive, motivational, physical—that might *possibly* make it either easier or harder for a child to perform well on each test item. After one such session, a woman who had taught learning-disabled children for ten years approached me and said, "I understand why you wanted us to do this. It makes perfect sense. But now I can't figure out what I've been doing for the past ten years." She explained that in her training she was primarily taught, "If a child gets these scores on these tests, you use these teaching materials." No one encouraged critical, logical thinking aimed at understanding in detail what the individual child could and could not do. And because her teachers were highly respected in their field, she had had no reason to question the truth or usefulness of the approach they had taught her. In fact, because they were so experienced and so famous, she assumed that any confusion she felt must be a sign of her own inadequacy. She guessed she wasn't smart enough to understand their reasons for working as they did.

I had had a similar experience some years earlier. Coming into the field of learning disabilities as a graduate student, I noticed that fully trained psychologists were writing reports that I could not understand. For instance, they would write that a learning-disabled child "can think concretely but not verbally." It took me some time to realize that the problem was in what the psychologists were writing: They wrote as though "concrete" and "verbal" were opposites, but they are not. A child may have concrete verbal skills such as being able to name "table," "chair," and "socks," and a child may have abstract verbal skills, such as being able to describe the difference between "liberty" and "justice." The terms "concrete" and "verbal" are not opposites, and the designated experts' reports were confusing because they wrote as though they were.

Writing about the trainer's pretense of knowing the truth, Ben Carniol relates a story that a social worker told him:

> Now the supervisor turns on me and says—what's the matter with you? Don't you know what to do?
>
> The thing is, the supervisor sometimes doesn't have the answer either. But instead of admitting it, the supervisor scares away the worker. After being treated that way, the worker learns not to ask again. Especially since it's the supervisor who evaluates the performance of the front-line worker.[1]

• *Some are biased, intellectually lazy, or not particularly intelligent.*

Glenna Atwood, a woman with Parkinson's disease, has written that a medical student "observed my tremor and asked me to walk. My walk was awkward, and my arm swing was almost nonexistent. His statement was cold and brief: "That isn't Parkinson's. The tremor is too fine. I'd say it's more likely to be a tumor on the brain." With that he left. I do not know his name, but whoever he is, and wherever he is, I hope he has learned a great deal more about diagnosing Parkinson's and dealing with patients.[2]

As with any group of people, some authorities do not think critically because they are not very intelligent or inquisitive, or they are strongly affected by their biases—or both. As Grant[3] points out, for instance, some ominous information about the Dalkon Shield intrauterine birth control device (IUD) was downplayed while the shield was vigorously promoted "as a technological marvel."[4] Two articles had appeared in a single issue of the journal *Obstetrics and Gynecology* in 1968. One was a report of the death, three days after her Dalkon Shield was inserted, of a young mother of four children. The other was a report on the advantages of IUDs. It is clear that there was disagreement within the medical community, and we have to wonder whether it was intellectual sloppiness, a bias in favor of technology, or other factors that led to minimizing of the possible dangers.

Similarly, was it sloppiness, anti-mother bias, or something else that led to the following: In an article about children who might be expected to develop emotional problems, the authors described the father of one such child by giving his age, his occupation, and the statement that he was "healthy." They described the same child's mother by giving her age and saying she was "nervous."[5] But later in the article, we learn that this father abused his child, who was terrified of him and cried as a result when talking about him. In spite of this dramatic evidence, the authors concluded that children like this can grow up normally—if their *mothers* treat them right. Because of the writers' lack of critical thinking, the father's shocking treatment of his child seems to have vanished when it was time for conclusions to be drawn.

When the authorities are researchers, surprisingly often they just don't think very deeply about the kinds of research questions they ask. For instance, because babies spend nine months inside their mother's body, it made a great deal of sense to explore the possibility that fetuses could be harmed by the mother's exposure to toxic substances. A great deal of such research has been done. But only now are researchers starting to pay much attention to the effect on babies of their *father's* exposure to toxic substances. Perhaps this is because we live in a culture in which mothers are more likely than fathers to be blamed for anything bad that happens to their children,[6] perhaps it is because the father's role in conception is brief and he has no role in gestation, and perhaps it is because as a society we have not wanted to know that workplaces (where fathers, more than mothers, are still *expected* to be) could be harmful to our health. Whatever the reason or reasons, an important research question was almost totally neglected. And now that the question is being more energetically explored, "Evidence is accumulating to implicate [fathers' exposure to] alcohol, drugs, smoking, and job-related poisons" in their children's "birth defects, cancer, growth retardation, and abnormal behavior."[7]

Palter and D'Argo of Greenpeace report another important case of researchers—through intellectual laziness or a bias toward looking at only certain kinds of causes for illness—asking only some of the relevant questions.[8] Between 1940 and 1993, they note, the rate of breast cancer in women increased dramatically, from 1 in 20 to 1 in 8. Although most of physicians' talk about breast cancer prevention and causes is focused on heredity, reproductive history, and diet, fewer than one-third of cases are explained by these factors.[9] An obvious research question would seem to be, "What possible causes have changed between 1940 and now as dramatically as the increase in breast cancer rates?" One reasonable answer is the amount of chemicals and toxins in our food, water, and environment, but the traditional medical and research enterprises have paid scant attention to these possibilities.[10] This is all the more disappointing because, even if women scrupulously controlled their reproductive patterns and their diet, as long as we cannot control our heredity and as long as the levels of toxic substances that surround us remain the same, far fewer than one-third of women likely to get breast cancer will be able to do anything to avoid it.[11]

Experts can do significant harm when they fail to think carefully before saying what their research proves. This was reflected in a large-scale study of psychologists, social workers, and psychiatrists that was aimed at investigating therapists' knowledge and attitudes about sexual assault victims who were their therapy clients.[12] In the summary at the beginning of their paper—the only part many readers look at—they say, "On the average, therapists . . . showed positive attitudes toward victims."[13] Positive attitudes include not blaming the victim for having been assaulted. However, those who read twelve pages into the article find that approximately 65 percent of the therapists use "treatment" techniques that involve blaming the client for the assaults, and eighteen pages into the article, that "sexual assault victim clients in this sample" were as likely to be treated by blaming as by nonblaming therapists.

This one study shows intellectual problems on the part of both the researchers and the experts whom they studied: Researchers are not always clear or consistent about what they claim their research proves, and many so-called experts either are not aware of the latest information relevant to their work or choose to ignore it. In this case, they were either unaware that victim-blaming is hurtful to the client or were determined to blame her anyway. With regard to the latter concern, anyone who has been sexually assaulted and goes to a therapist for help has a worryingly high chance of ending up with one who believes the assault to be her or his own fault.

Another type of inadequate thinking in regard to research questions is simplistic thinking. For example, there has been a long-standing debate about whether men are naturally and inevitably more aggressive than women. There are far-reaching implications of this debate, because if males' violence is natural and inevitable, then some people would want to excuse men who batter their wives or sexually assault their students, and some would argue that there is no point in trying to avoid wars, because men have to express their aggression somehow.

Much of the research on this topic has been in response to the question, "Does the 'male hormone' testosterone *cause* aggression?" and some studies suggest that the answer is, "Yes, in some ways, under some circumstances, using some definitions of 'aggression.'" When we think of hormones affecting behavior, most of us assume that people cannot do very much to control hormonally based behavior. So if the research enterprise had stopped there, it would have left the general impression that men cannot help being violent.

What most scientists failed to do until recently, however, was to ask the reverse question: "Can aggressive behavior lead to a rise in testosterone?" Researchers exploring that cause-effect relationship have now shown that behaving aggressively can increase one's testosterone level. So, too, can stress (such as the stress from being stuck by a needle to have one's hormone levels measured). For many of us, that sheds a very different light on the question of whether men can control their aggressive behavior, for behaving in less dominant and aggressive ways may lower a hormone that is a contributing factor to aggressive behavior. But we aren't likely to consider the subtler possibilities as long as the experts explore only the simplistic hormones-produce-behavior kinds of sequences.

Conscientious critical thinking by authorities also involves trying to overcome our biases, asking ourselves if our biases or our system's attitudes about sex, race, age, disability, sexual orientation, social class, or physical attractiveness might be clouding our thinking and interfering with our ability to provide good service. For example, in an appalling story of still-common racist bias, a white employment counselor spent five full minutes suggesting to a Black man a series of jobs involving hard physical labor that he might pursue. Finally, the man handed the counselor his resume and pointed out that he had a master's degree in business administration and that his last job had been as an account manager at an advertising agency. The doctor who failed to diagnose the eighty-nine-year-old woman as having AIDS was guilty of ageism, sexism, and maybe "lookism," or prejudice against people who don't match conventional ideals of attractiveness. In still another illustration of author- ities' bias limiting their thinking, a woman went to her physi- cian because she had terrible menstrual cramps. He fired a volley of questions at her regarding her use of birth control— "Do you use it? No?! Why not?! After all, you *are* unmarried, aren't you? Has anyone ever told you about the birth control options that are available?"—without pausing for breath. Final- ly, she interrupted him to say, "I am a lesbian, so I don't really need birth control."

- *They are not taught or encouraged to listen with a questioning mind.*

In *many* jobs, including the professions and government ser- vices, spending time listening to and supporting the con- sumer is *not* taught; in fact, it may even be discouraged. And because authorities are rarely encouraged to *listen* to the con- sumer, they can miss information that is essential if they truly want to help. My friend Gillian worked as a psychiatric nurse on a hospital ward with teenagers who were dependent on drugs or alcohol. She is warm and open, so during the groups she ran for these patients, they often described experiences they had never disclosed to anyone else. Frequently, the dis- closures were about having been sexually abused. Her chief psychiatrist called her on the carpet, saying, "These kids don't disclose this material when they meet with me for individual therapy, so you must be forcing them to talk before they are ready!" That was a clear message to Gillian that she should stop being such a good listener. Although she realized her boss was embarrassed because his patients hadn't felt com- fortable confiding in him, Gillian says that she felt tempted to stop listening as a result of his disapproval. For years before that, of course, she had learned that to question someone in authority was troublemaking, impolite, antisocial, and cer- tainly unfeminine. In spite of all that pressure, Gillian resist- ed changing her behavior, but it took a great deal of courage for her to do so.

- *They don't know what they don't know.*

As briefly mentioned in Chapter 4, for a variety of reasons, experts sometimes aren't even aware of what they don't know. Sometimes this is because, as discussed, they receive their training from teachers who act as though the material they are presenting is all one needs to know. And when one's teachers take this attitude, it may not occur to us that there is something more, or we may be afraid to point out that there may be more, or both. As a result, when experts cannot explain a problem based on what they already happen to know, instead of looking for another explanation, they may assume there is no solution.

Remember that my family doctor told me that my low energy level was due to the fact that I was forty-five and that, if I would eat less, I could lose weight, and my energy would increase. I protested that when I ate *less*, my already low energy dropped even lower. He shrugged. Perhaps it never occurred to him to say, "I don't know everything" and "Logically, this *doesn't* make sense, so there must be an explanation we haven't found yet." Perhaps no one ever urged him to consider and acknowledge openly the possibility that an explanation could lie outside his arena of familiarity. I suspect that if my doctor were simply reading a newspaper article about this issue in his home and could forget that as a doctor he is expected to have the answers to all health-related questions, he wouldn't find it hard to recognize that the puzzle was missing a piece. I know him to be intelligent and caring, and his inability to think critically and questioningly about my situation seems to reflect his need to come up with explanations *only* within the framework of what he learned in medical school. This is particularly perplexing, because he has avoided the traditional, detached, even dismissive attitude many doctors have toward patients. How sad that he could not overcome this other limitation.

In my own work, I see many examples of experts not knowing that they don't know. I have often heard therapists claim that a child is having trouble because of having no father, no "adult male role model" at home. Many researchers have worked on what they call the harm of "father absence," and single mothers have often told me that experts have warned them that they cannot raise emotionally healthy children without an adult male in the home.[14] They are cautioned that their daughters will become promiscuous because of looking desperately for a father-substitute and that their sons will become homosexual because of having no idea how to "be male." But father-absence researchers have primarily dealt with families that are fatherless through divorce or desertion by the father, of which society disapproves. Perhaps it is not surprising, then, that the "findings" were that father absence hurts children. That provides more ammunition for criticizing those fathers or criticizing the wives who presumably drove them to divorce or desertion. Researchers have virtually excluded families whose fathers are physically absent owing to work, such as careers in the navy or simply the choice to spend endless hours at the office or elsewhere. Because society hasn't been much concerned about work taking fathers away from their children, most father-absence researchers have labeled only certain types of absence as problems. It may not even occur to them to label as "father-absent" those homes in which the father is away long hours because of work; thus, they do not even know that they are failing to study an important group. Fearful single mothers might feel less apprehensive if they knew that the experts have ignored the harm that might come to children because their fathers are never home due to work—or obsession with sports or gambling, and so on. But the fact that millions of women have raised well-adjusted children virtually alone has been lost as father-absence researchers failed to notice those essentially "father-absent" homes that are socially condoned.

- *They can get away with it.*

Some authorities and experts will do, or not do, whatever they can without being held accountable for it. Precisely because consumers are reluctant to ask questions, the authority's privilege includes rarely being challenged, and although some people in that role feel badly that their clients hesitate to question them, others are relieved to avoid the bother. In an article about this reluctance among physicians' patients, Ubelacker quotes a sixty-four-year-old woman who comes away from appointments with her doctor "feeling angry, confused and powerless" because "He never tells me anything." But the woman is "horrified at her daughter's suggestion that she push him for more information. 'He's a doctor. You don't question doctors'."[15] Ubelacker claims that this attitude is more prevalent among older people than among baby boomers, but many boomers hold the same attitude; and even those who do not are often daunted and frustrated by some doctors' continuing arrogance or evasiveness when patients muster the courage to press them for answers.

Laypeople often assume that authorities surely cannot get away with much, because their supervisors will exercise quality control, there are laws and ethical standards to protect consumers, and those experts who are professionals have discipline bodies that keep their members in line. It is probably true that authorities who feel that Big Brother is watching are less likely to slide into lazy thinking or unquestioning execution of their tasks than those who know that no one will notice. As Kate Rounds pointed out in her recent *Ms.* magazine article about nurses, at least in hospitals, a clear-thinking nurse may catch the error of a doctor who mistakenly orders that a patient be given ten milligrams of a drug rather than one.[16]

For so many services, however, there are few or no safeguards. And often, there's not much point in filing a complaint, even if there is a watchdog group. The Better Business Bureaus in some cities are terrific, for instance, but in others, if you're the only customer to go to the trouble to file a complaint against a particular business, they won't take action until they receive several other complaints about that firm.

Perhaps because lawyers work in the "justice" system, we may be surprised to learn that the bar associations that are supposed to handle complaints against lawyers sometimes protect the lawyers rather than the clients they have harmed. Consider the case of the lawyer for one party who announced in open court that the client on the opposing side was "notorious in her home city for her mendacity" (her lying). That lawyer had never met the woman nor seen any evidence that this was so (as indeed it was not), so his claim could be interpreted as evidence of sloppy thinking and arguing, as simple belligerence, or as both. When the woman filed a complaint with his bar association, the association never gave her any indication that they had asked the attorney to present evidence to support his name-calling. Instead, it simply notified the woman that they had dismissed her complaint and taken no action.

Another recent instance involved the egregious failures of the watchdog groups for three different professions to hold their members accountable for their misconduct in a single case. A man I'll call Herbert had petitioned the court for custody of his young daughter, because her mother was severely neglecting and emotionally abusing her. Herbert's lawyer, Mr. Nurn, suggested several people to do the psychological assessment of the family members to Mr. Stone, the lawyer for Herbert's ex-wife. Mr. Stone rejected each suggestion, remarking in one case that the therapist was a close personal friend of his. Repeatedly, Mr. Stone stated that the assessment should be done by Dr. Martin, the psychiatrist who had served as mediator for Herbert and his ex-wife. Because Dr. Martin had made snide remarks about Herbert's child, Mr. Nurn explained this in a letter to Mr. Stone, rejecting the suggestion of using Dr. Martin again.

When the lawyers asked a judge to order that an assessment be done, the judge asked, "Who will do the assessment?" Mr. Stone quickly suggested, "How about Louise Sludge?" Because Ms. Sludge was a social worker who had done much child custody work, and Mr. Nurn feared that the judge would consider him and his clients troublemakers if they refused, he agreed. Well into the assessment process, Herbert learned that his ex-wife's lawyer and Dr. Martin had founded the clinic where Ms. Sludge was employed, had recently served on its board of directors, and had done a great deal of teaching with Ms. Sludge. Herbert told Ms. Sludge of his wish that Dr. Martin not be involved in the assessment, because he was clearly biased. In spite of this, Ms. Sludge discussed the case with Dr. Martin.

Most disturbing of all, she did this without so much as asking Herbert's permission to speak to him. According to their professional ethical standards, both Dr. Martin and Ms. Sludge are required to obtain written consent from patients before discussing their cases *at all* with anyone else.

Herbert filed complaints against Mr. Stone with the local bar association on the grounds that he had failed to disclose the potential conflict of interest when suggesting in court that Ms. Sludge do the assessment. The bar association took no action against Mr. Stone. In fact, months after the complaint was thrown out, Herbert learned that the bar association itself had acted improperly: It seems that Mr. Stone was a member of the association's executive committee, and *by their own rules* (which were never shown to Herbert), when a complaint is filed against a member of its executive, the association is required to call in an outside investigator to deal with the case. They did not do so but merely had one of their regular people— over whom Mr. Stone had some executive power—handle it.

Herbert also filed complaints against Dr. Martin with the psychiatric association and against Ms. Sludge with the social workers' association. The most important feature of those complaints was that neither professional had obtained Herbert's consent before discussing the case with each other. Both "discipline bodies" dismissed the cases against their members and took no action. Soon afterward in a newsletter sent to its members, the social workers' association warned its members against doing the kind of thing Ms. Sludge had done (without mentioning her name), so they clearly knew it was wrong.

And in one more case, DiManno reports that the man acting as judge in a police disciplinary hearing acknowledged his friendship with the accused when announcing the very light penalty he was imposing. The light penalty was for the policeman having coerced a prostitute into having sex with him by threatening to arrest her if she did not.[17] DiManno remarks, "How convenient, having a friend in the judge. In any other quasi-judicial procedure, this might have been construed as a conflict of interest. But some cops march to their own rules." When not only sloppy thinking but even blatantly unethical behavior is protected by the groups that are supposed to be watchdogs, it is no wonder that so many authorities continue to act as they wish.

Even where good watchdog groups exist, clients may hesitate to file complaints because they know they may be brutally cross-examined if a hearing is held.[18] Furthermore, for those who file complaints, crucial evidence can be hard to obtain. As Kramer writes,

> Were [doctors'] records independently constructed and open freely to colleagues, the truth . . . might be more widely circulated. Were there . . . a device like a flight recorder in every operating room—say an always-running video camera and microphone—private events might be publicly reconstructed if the need arose.[19]

I've suggested something similar for therapy—take a tape recorder to your sessions, play the tapes later for others, and see whether they think your therapist is really helping you, putting you down, controlling you, and the like. But until such practices are common, gathering convincing evidence to support complaints remains difficult.

• *Power defines truth (and so, often, does arrogance).*

First you say things our way and then we'll listen to you.
—Robert Pirsig[20]

The defining and streamlining of science and truth by an elite group has a long history: In Galileo's time, for instance, the powerful intellectuals believed fervently that the earth was the center of the universe, and Galileo was forced to recant his announcement that the earth was *not* the center. Although to the consumer, an authority anywhere in the hierarchy of a system seems powerful, most authorities work under someone else's control, and most experts are sensitive to the approval or disapproval of others in their field. As human beings, authorities and experts cannot help but be affected by the beliefs and prejudices of the powerful people in their areas. As a result, researchers deciding which topics to study and which research questions to ask may be influenced by their awareness of what the elite regard as the important issues and the right approaches.[21] Other factors that shape research and claims about truth include the projects that agencies and foundations are inclined to fund and the topics, attitudes, and theories that are considered important enough to justify raises and promotions. That is why, until recent years, most psychological research was conducted on white males: Women and people of color of both sexes were simply not considered important enough to study.[22] That is also why the research that was done on nondominant groups tended to support claims that those groups were inferior, such as studies of Blacks' supposedly inferior intelligence or of women's supposed emotional instability.

Robert Pirsig vividly describes how it feels to voice an opinion or interpretation that conflicts with the doctrine accepted by the powerful: "you have hit an invisible wall of prejudice. Nobody on the inside of that wall is ever going to listen to you; not because what you say isn't true, but solely because you have been identified as outside that wall," a wall he suggests calling a "cultural immune system" that shuts dissenters not only out of arenas of power but even away from fair hearings.[23] In doing the research for my recent book on women in academia, I was astonished to discover how widespread is the tendency for powerful professors to usurp the right to decide what is legitimate or important knowledge.[24] When I had applied for a teaching job in one university's psychology department, a member of the search committee asked me, "When are you going to stop doing research on women and start doing *important* work?" None of the other committee members objected to his question. And younger colleagues have described similar, recent experiences to me.

At no less an institution than the federally funded National Institute of Mental Health (NIMH), physician Dr. Jean Hamilton told her boss that she had found evidence that certain drugs affect women and men quite differently. This was extremely important, because research was often done on drugs' effects on men only, and then the drugs were prescribed for women according to the guidelines developed for men.

Hamilton noted that hormonal differences appeared to interact with drugs, and she thought those possible interactions should be scientifically investigated. But her supervisor thought he already knew the truth. Hamilton writes, "I was informed that there couldn't be an important clinical effect, because, if there were, we'd already know about it. So much for the scientific method." When she pressed him on the issue, she says, her "lab chief was becoming visibly nervous: maybe they had missed something."[25] However, he discouraged her from publishing a paper on the topic.

> When it came time to renew my fellowship . . . I was informed that these were low priority topics. A male colleague in my lab said that what I was doing (studying drugs in women) wasn't even pharmacology.[26]

Later on, Hamilton reports, another man at NIMH pressured her former boss to release data that proved her correct, but her name was never listed as a co-author on the papers eventually published from that laboratory and based on work she had helped to do.

The assumption that the powerful know the truth affects people as they move up through the ranks of power. Too often, when the less powerful become more powerful, they forget that they are fallible. As Rounds reports in her article about hospital nurses,

> a disagreement about the dosage of a medication erupts between a doctor and nurse. "It's one milligram, not ten milligrams," the nurse insists. The nurse, it turns out, is right. "Some doctors don't want to listen," she says. . . . "When doctors are new, we try to mold them. They get arrogant and anxious when they don't know as much." Another nurse puts it this way: "We have to teach young doctors. When the residents get more confident, you can't approach them."[27]

- *They are protecting their territory.*

One of the specific ways in which the powerful control how truth is defined is by protecting their territory, often by speaking in demeaning ways about everyone who doesn't work in the same field or profession or who did not have the same training as they. They act as though, if you come from outside their field, you have no right to think critically about what they do. At worst, they imply that you aren't intelligent enough to understand what they know and what they do. "What *we* don't know or believe is wrong," they suggest. Some authorities do this because they fear that, if word gets out that *anyone* can understand their work, then they might lose their jobs: "If I *explain* how to work the computer system I set up, people will see that it's really pretty easy to understand, and then they may feel that I'm expendable." But if the rest of us accept that attitude, we are no better than those who choose *any* authorities and unquestioningly accept whatever they might say. One consequence of this attitude is that, increasingly, technical tasks are valued over humane ones that "anyone" can do: Nurse Patricia Moore explained how nurses often responded when she asked them to describe their work.[28] They would say, "I inserted the needle for the intravenous feeding. Then I adjusted the drip to make sure the fluid was going in at the proper rate. Then I took the patient's blood pressure and checked the heart monitor." Having watched the nurses perform the procedures they later described, Moore observed that they rarely mentioned that they had explained procedures to patients, reassured them, patted their hands, or asked if they needed anything. When she asked the nurses why they hadn't reported those activities, their replies were along the lines of, "I thought you wanted me to describe the work." For many nurses, "work" has increasingly come to mean only technical procedures, because those are more likely than customer service, patient care, and humane behavior to be considered worthy of being regarded with dignity and respect. They are more like what the doctor does.

Many professionals support each other in defining truth, making it extremely hard for the consumer to find out what really is the case.

When second opinions are required [from doctors] for insurance plans, nearly a fifth of them, according to some research, fail to confirm initial recommendations. But patients once in pursuit of cure seem either to grow eager for surgery, or else to be eagerly directed by advisers; about 70 percent of negative second opinions in one study got changed once again by *third* opinions. In the end, second opinions cause the rate of surgical intervention to decline only about 8 percent.[29]

Another consequence of allowing the powerful to define truth is that access to information about important issues is often limited, even to experts working in the same field. During my undergraduate and graduate training in psychology, I read books by the brilliant psychoanalyst Erik Erikson, who developed the theory of identity crisis and made many insightful contributions to our understanding of human behavior. In one book, he claimed that he had shown through a large research study that "Boys build towers, and girls build enclosures" when given toys and blocks. He went on from that report to draw two important, sweeping conclusions. First, he said, this proves that, because females have wombs and males have erectible penises, females perceive and organize space differently from males. (If he is right about this, we would expect that no woman would ever design a building like the Empire State Building, and no man could design the Hollywood Bowl or a football stadium.) Second, he said that a woman cannot acquire a solid sense of her identity until she has established a relationship with a man who will fill her inner space. There are, of course, profound implications of that claim for women's understanding of what will make us happy.

Erikson's claim about his research is so well known and widely believed that I have heard people say knowingly at cocktail parties, "You know, boys build towers and girls build enclosures," and it is sometimes cited as fact in popular literature as well as by professional therapists.[30] Furthermore, unbelievable though it may seem in this era, I have often heard therapists say that some of their women patients are unhappy because they are not willing to devote enough of their energy to the man who "fills their inner space."

Years after reading that report in Erikson's book, his conclusions floated across my mind, and I suddenly realized how important were the implications he had drawn from his single study.[31] I went to the library to read in a mental health journal the full report of the tower-enclosure research that he had only partially described in his book. Until I read the article, I hadn't questioned the accuracy of Erikson's description of his data in his book, and therefore I had never questioned the conclusions he had drawn about sex differences on that basis. Because I have great respect for Erikson, I was upset by what I found in the article. There are too many problems with his study to describe them all here, although I have done so elsewhere,[32] but I shall present two of the most egregious ones here. First, without knowing anything about statistics, anyone could see in his article that almost all of the children of *both* sexes built enclosures. Very few children of either sex built towers, although of the tiny fraction who built towers, slightly more were built by boys than by girls. In spite of this, Erikson freely refers to towers as the male structure and to enclosures as the female one. Second, in drawing conclusions from his (misinterpreted) data, Erikson got his physiology wrong. The uterus is not really an inner space. Most of the time, it looks like a folded flapjack. And finally, when I redid Erikson's experiment, my results certainly did not support the claim that boys build towers and girls build enclosures.

If Erikson's research is so flawed, how did his claims about it acquire the status of truth? I think it is partly because Erikson is highly respected for some of his good work, so many people are reluctant to question anything he does or it doesn't occur to them that someone so insightful about certain things could be wrong about others. Another important factor is that his original research paper was published in a journal that is not read by the most hardnosed researchers, who would be likely to question his methods and interpretations of his data. Thus, the "evidence" for his claims was not likely to be scrutinized by the people most inclined to question it.

• *Accepted doctrine is misleading.*

Allowing the powerful to define truth often inhibits authorities from thinking critically about accepted doctrine. As Sylvester points out, a therapist who believes in a particular theory may be trapped "into testing irrelevant or inaccurate information."[33] Imagine that a man who has just lost his job tells his therapist that he feels depressed. A therapist who believes that the fear of being castrated is a major motivator for men, as Freud taught, will probably ask the patient such questions as, "When you were a child, did your father ever catch you masturbating and threaten to castrate you?" rather than focusing more productively on such questions as "What are your greatest fears and your greatest actual problems in relation to losing your job?" And a therapist who believes that women enjoy suffering will encourage a woman who has lost her job to "admit" that she really wanted to be fired.

A few years ago, I read a newspaper article about a nurse who ran self-help groups for widows. The groups were remarkably effective in alleviating the women's depression and getting them reinvolved in living. When she tried to organize self-help groups for widowers, though, she found that they were ineffective. With great delight, she announced that what worked for the men was to pair them with widows! Although we might be pleased to hear that the men cheered up, we also have to realize that the nurse's beliefs may have clouded her view of what would help the men the most in the long run. Because men are not encouraged to talk to other men when they feel upset, nor to identify and cope with their emotions, they were relieved to be paired with widows, who as women had been encouraged to help men deal with feelings. That might have helped the men, but it made it unlikely that they would ever learn important skills for dealing with emotions, and it also perpetuated the pattern of making women responsible for the whole realm of feelings and relationships. Had the well-meaning nurse thought critically about the consequences of perpetuating the men's stereotypic, learned style of coping, she might have chosen to help them learn to express their feelings (even to other men). This might have been better for them in the long run than hoping to find women who understand and meet their needs without their ever having to figure out and say what they feel.

- *Those within the system but not at the top may be punished for critical thinking.*

As described in Chapter 4, if we see that the emperor is wearing no clothes and dare to say that, we can be swiftly and harshly punished. In a recent, important case, a skilled, high-level employee applied her critical thinking skills to the work going on around her, realized that something was very wrong, and spoke up about it. The results for her were disastrous:

> Margot O'Toole . . . faced persecution after blowing the whistle on her employer at MIT [Massachusetts Institute of Technology]. While working as a research scientist in 1985, O'Toole found it impossible to replicate the results of experiments conducted by the head of the lab. She tried to get him to retract his incorrect scientific claims, but her superior refused. O'Toole was then labeled vindictive and was threatened with legal action. Other scientists who expressed an interest in hiring her were advised not to. She was accused of mental instability. Moreover, as a result of her decision to speak out, O'Toole was forced to work in total professional isolation and ostracism.[34]

It is possible to persist in a questioning attitude in the face of such treatment, but it can take years to get positive results, and those results may drain one's energy, use up enormous amounts of time, or never even come. In O'Toole's case, "she refused to succumb to the bullying. Eventually, an investigation began and the cover-up proved unsuccessful. *Five years later*, the paper was retracted."[35]

- *Pressures due to time, workload, and limited resources restrict critical thinking.*

Many authorities struggle to keep up with their daily workload, given their staff and other resources. It can be daunting for them not only to think of doing what their job description mandates but, *in addition*, to invest time and effort in wondering whether they are doing their job as well and efficiently as possible, whether they are helping the people they are supposed to serve, and whether the "truths" they take as givens are really based on evidence and sound reasoning. And because doing critical thinking feels like job overload, it is not surprising that many develop enormous emotional resistance to thinking critically about their work. As Atwood has written in her book about Parkinson's disease, "My family doctor and the neurologist had so many other illnesses to deal with. The question kept recurring in my mind: How much time do they really have to keep up with the latest on one disease—Parkinson's?"[36]

Speaking as a psychologist who has worked during most of my career with physicians, I can attest to the difficulty of trying to keep up with the sheer volume of published material about the various conditions we might have to recognize and deal with. For instance, at one time I specialized in children's learning disabilities, but a child I might be asked to assess for learning disabilities might have been performing poorly in school because of a brain tumor, high anxiety, petit mal seizures, or schizophrenia. The parents might be caring, loving people, or they might be abusing their child, setting unreasonably high expectations about school performance, or focusing on the child's academic difficulty to avoid a whole range of personal problems of their own. It is not humanly possible to read all of the literature on all of these topics, and some professionals don't even try. But even those who do may feel overwhelmed by the prospect of both digesting all of that material and applying a questioning, analytic attitude to what they read. And if we are doing research of our own, we may be too caught up in that work to inspect others' research reports with care.

A recent dispute about the usefulness of mammograms to diagnose breast cancer in its early stages has been clouded by the lack of critical thinking that went into a major research project, and at least one physician suggests that that lack was due to pressure on the researchers to rush their results into print and to the lack of money for such research.[37] In regard to a massive study suggesting that mammograms were not very effective in early identification of breast cancer, Dr. Howard Seiden explains that there were deficiencies in the quality of X-ray equipment and training of technicians and physicians used in the study. He also believes that some of the personnel were unwilling to take constructive criticism. But to change all that

> would have meant millions of extra dollars and perhaps a year or two or three of extra set-up time. No, that would not do. It's a publish or perish world in research land. Therefore, the thinking goes, valuable time would be wasted in prolonging the start-up phase. There would be nothing to publish for years.[38]

If we give such researchers the benefit of the doubt, we can understand that the prospect of speeding up the discovery of cures for ill people could impel them to rush through their research. If we take a more cynical view, we have to worry that some researchers' need to amass a list of published articles so that they can win raises, promotions, and fame is what hurries them along and limits their critical thinking.

Sometimes the cynical attitude is clearly appropriate, as when financial greed inhibits critical thinking—especially when people's lives are at stake, as in this case:

> As pacemakers improved, daring companies with the "right" next innovation fattened, and conservatively managed companies got eaten. And an increasing range of patients became candidates for pacemakers. Recently, government hearings have shown that the pacemaker's popularity has exceeded its appropriate uses—that perhaps a fifth of pacemaker patients might do as well without them.[39]

In this case, the demand for money overcame some manufacturers' and physicians' inclination to think skeptically. Kramer's report was published nearly ten years ago, and one hopes that pacemakers are developed, tested, and implanted with greater care. But it is significant that financial greed helped shape the definition of knowledge: the newest pacemaker was assumed to be the best.

WHAT AUTHORITIES HAVE TO GAIN BY THINKING CRITI-
CALLY

What authorities stand to gain from asking questions and from being responsive to our clients' questions is the tremendous relief that comes from dropping the pretense of perfection and omniscience. Even the most powerful of authorities can feel insecure about their limitations: "Judge [Henry] Steinberg writes about . . . the sense of insecurity that goes along with being newly appointed to the bench . . . [and] the gnawing doubts about whether a decision is correct."[40] Sometimes, those who are the most knowledgeable are willing to entertain questions without becoming defensive, because they feel secure in their extensive knowledge—but this is not always the case, because those with the most knowledge are sometimes those with the most power to lose and the greatest fear of sharing their power. But when authorities are willing to question and to listen to questions, we can invigorate our stale practices and revise procedures that, at some level, we have known weren't working well. A great example of this openness was my uncle, William Karchmer, a lawyer who was dearly loved and appreciated by his clients because he taught them and described their options and the pros and cons of each one, rather than just telling them what to do. When they left his office, they took with them an understanding of the whole picture and had some genuine control. This was a true working partnership. And that is a gratifying way to live.

7

What Limits Consumers' Critical Thinking?

Coming from outside the system, consumers are often free from some of the impediments to critical thinking that plague authorities, such as fear of losing one's job because of complaining about *their* system. However, many factors tend to silence consumers who might otherwise question the claims of authorities and experts, ranging from the authoritative manner of presentation, to lack of support for such behavior, to fears. Owing to the portrayal of authorities as so much more knowledgeable than the public, many consumers consider it normal to feel uncomfortable in their presence. This attitude makes us unlikely to wonder why we passively accept the ways they (mis)treat us, because when we feel uneasy in their presence, we assume that the fault is ours instead of, for instance, that they are failing to answer our direct inquiries.

Although self-help groups can do a great deal of good, I believe that their popularity partly reflects the public's preference for asking questions of their peers rather than pressing authorities to do what they are supposed to do. This is reflected in one of Glenna Atwood's chapter titles, "Support Groups: Where You Learn What Your Doctor Hasn't Time To Tell You."[1] The presumably busy doctor is absolved of the obligation to provide patients the information they need.

We now look at factors that specifically inhibit consumers' critical thinking.

- *Experts act as though what they say is indisputable and as though to question them is wrong.*

Experts' use of jargon was mentioned in Chapter 2 as a major mystifier of consumers, and so, too, is the authoritative *manner* in which they speak. Their manner often conveys the message, "Don't question me or think critically about what I say, or I'll help you even less than I am now!" From their attitude, we as consumers sense that to question them is somehow wrong and could reduce our chances of getting the services we need from them. We also learn from experience that it might make them very angry.

When we go to a doctor or pick up an advice book or apply for Workers' Compensation, we don't assume that to obtain as much help as possible, we need first to become experts ourselves on the procedures and the material in that field. And, of course, we shouldn't *have* to do that. Certainly, the experts rarely educate us about their work. The more awe-inspiring and high-status the authority or system is, the more we assume that those in power have the power *because* they know so much and will do what is right and what is necessary to help us. One of the most striking lessons I learned in my work was that neuropsychologists, people who study how the brain affects our behavior, are not all incredibly brilliant. Many of us tend to believe that people who *study* the brain *are* "brainy," and that was what I initially assumed. One year, I had to give a lecture about sex differences in the brain, but I knew very little about the subject. I phoned a colleague in another city, asked him to recommend some good articles, and sat down to read the lengthy, detailed chapter that he recommended as "the best work on the subject." For days, I felt totally inadequate to the task, because the author wrote with such self-assurance, but I was having great trouble following his logic as he interpreted one research study after another. I assumed that I was simply too stupid to comprehend such high-level thinking. But then, thank goodness, I reached the line where the author said we know that women have poor "spatial abilities," because there have been no women chess champions. That was my "Aha!" moment. I knew that there were a host of reasons for that sex difference, including the attitude that chess was a more appropriate game for males than for females and the fact that learning and playing chess requires long periods of time to concentrate totally on the task—something few women have been free to do unless the task has been taking care of other people. As soon as I saw that the chess example was not good scientific evidence, I relaxed, gained more confidence about my own thinking ability, and went back and began the whole article again. This time, as I read, I assumed that my trouble in following some of the author's arguments might be due to *his* faulty reasoning.

I think it was relatively easy to spot that author's faults because he wasn't physically present, and he did not wield life-or-death power over me. But as Kramer observes, when facing authorities who do have such power, we want to believe they really know their stuff and will help us. We know we probably cannot save ourselves, so we depend on them:

> Their [surgeons'] successes are painful enough to evoke quizzical responses even in those they heal. In the office, their work fosters such feelings of dependency that seriously ill patients may imagine they're talking to someone other than the surgeon altogether, someone especially protective. The dads they had when they were small. The Pope. Or just that generic authoritative figure, Doc.[2]

As a result of that awe and dependency, combined with our fear when we are ill or injured, few of us think critically about which doctor to choose. At those times, we may panic (and with reason, if we need immediate help), and we may fear the consequences if we check out other doctors and then want to return to the first one, who may by then be angry or too busy.

> [Surgical] patients rarely ask about price, rarely comparison shop, and rarely even seek second opinions before accepting their surgeons' advice. Patients go, and trust. [And in some systems, there *is* nowhere else to go, so why think critically?]. . . . Not only don't patients shop around for price or question their surgeons' verdicts much, but patients also don't often select their surgeons on the basis of technical excellence. Stearne's patients, whenever I asked them, seemed to have chosen him on the basis of impressions built upon much trust and little knowledge. They looked him up—yes, in the yellow pages—and liked him when they met him. . . . Or he saved a neighbor's life when the neighbor had something a few years ago. Or he took care of them when they were delivered to the emergency room, injured, so why switch now?[3]

Furthermore, questioning might turn up information that would impel you to take action that you feel too drained or rushed to take, such as switching to another lawyer and going through the whole history all over again, paying the new lawyer to read your entire file, and then maybe finding out that the new one is no better than the one you left.

The same dependent status that makes us hesitate to shop around also makes us reluctant to question the "helper" we ultimately choose. We sense that, with many, if we want their help, we had better seem wholeheartedly to support their view of the truth.

Being an authority in one field makes some people feel they have carte blanche to make authoritative pronouncements about anything at all. An infamous example of this was reported in a newspaper article headlined "Why does a scholarly journal publish prejudice passed off as science?" The journalist Morris Wolfe described how some scientists speak and write with great self-assurance, even when the topic is light-years away from their area of expertise. As Wolfe notes, "If Auntie Em or Uncle Gord make ignorant remarks about blacks or gays or whoever, we can do a number of things—argue, jolly them along, walk away, move on to another subject and so on."[4] But suppose, he continues that Uncle Gord is a university professor who writes that the reason Marc Lepine murdered fourteen Montreal women was that "Lepine's mother was a feminist, ambitious in her career, destructive to her children."[5] This is what Gordon Freeman, professor of chemistry at the University of Alberta, wrote in 1990 in the *Canadian Journal of Physics*! In the same article, Freeman reports that he actually *chose not* to conduct a systematic, controlled study because that would have created an artificial situation. Instead, he writes, he talked with students himself, and on that basis he concluded that mothers are to blame for the ills of society. One illustration of Freeman's absurd standards for deciding what is true can be found in his presentation of "evidence" of mothers' harm. His "proof" is an anecdote about two premedical students who said that physicians could bill Medicare for patients who did not exist, and whose mothers worked for pay!

In Freeman's case, the energy and efforts of people who thought critically and then voiced their objections led the journal editors to publish an apology, but often such appallingly bad "science" goes unquestioned. These examples should encourage us to remember that sometimes there is no justification for authorities' self-assured claims and that our own logical, problem-solving skills may be better than theirs. It may help to keep in mind the joke: "What do you call the person who graduates at the bottom of the medical school class?" Answer: "Doctor." At least half of all professionals in every field graduated in the bottom half of their class, and the same is probably true of researchers who make pronouncements about truth, auto mechanics, computer salespeople, and so on. Keeping that in view should make us feel less intimidated in the face of authorities' self-assured, silencing treatment.

• *They fear our power, and we fear our own power.*

Another reason for the rarity of consumers' critical thinking is that, once we start to ask questions rather than just accepting what we are told, we may become dangerous to the system. We might uncover errors—or worse—in authorities' beliefs or procedures. And those who don't want to help us will fear us when we speak up. By speaking politely and making it clear that we assume they wish to help us, we can sometimes minimize the degree to which *some* experts will feel threatened when we question them; for others, though, the reality that our questions could ultimately reduce their power, make them seem less special and important, or cause them to lose their jobs is so great that they cannot see beyond their fear. And another hard reality is that that fear will lead some to blame or punish us by not giving us the services they are supposed to provide.

Many people who know or sense this danger have understandably been silenced, because it is natural to try to placate those whose help we seek. But it is good to remember that, when it looks like we won't get that help from the person with whom we are dealing, we may have little else to lose (beyond some energy and time) and perhaps even something to gain by questioning what they are doing.

- *We don't want to be rude.*

A principle perpetuated by many authorities is that it is rude to question authorities. It's not nice, for instance, to assume that a doctor doesn't have your interests at heart. After all, we know that they take the Hippocratic Oath, in which they vow to work "for the good of the sick." But where does that leave us when we read about the sky-high rate of disease, disease *caused by doctors* (called "iatrogenic disease"),[6] or about teachers who care more about disciplining than about teaching our child, or about lawyers for whom maintaining their old-boy network with other lawyers takes precedence over protecting our interests? I felt the power of the notion that it is rude to question authorities when a close relative was in the hospital and his doctors were slow in telling him the results of important tests. I was in the process of writing this book, urging others to question authorities when it seems important to do so, but I knew that, although I had every right to question the professionals, if one of them considered me rude or insolent for doing so, that could affect the care he gave my relative. And if you are willing to ask questions but think of them after the doctors leave, you telephone them at the risk of being considered a pest.

We are damned either way: If we are questioning, challenging, suspicious of the experts, we are considered paranoid and angry, and we risk reprisals (the teacher will punish our child, the doctor will stop returning our phone calls), which leave us in an even *worse* position than before. If we don't question, we remain mystified, uninformed, powerless—our hands are tied. And if, heaven forbid, we challenge more than one person or institution, they may get together and portray us as crazy people whose only aim is to make trouble and whose concerns should, therefore, be ignored.

Such factors as the questioner's age, race, sex, and social class play powerful roles in determining what is rude in these situations. Often, older people have stronger beliefs about what is polite and appropriate in dealing with authorities: Atwood points out that, when physicians were investigating some problems she was having, she knows that she

> should have asked for more information, but my generation has been conditioned not to question the doctor; we've learned to sit and agree to do what the doctor tells us to do. . . . I realize that some patients really may not want to know any more than what the doctor tells them, but I was anxious to educate myself about this illness that had taken up residence in my body.[7]

Despite her own wish for more information, then, this older woman was silenced by her fear of being considered rude. As we grow older, many of us also can see that we may need the help of doctors increasingly over the years, and that is all the more reason that we may become more reluctant to question them.

Indeed, any individual or group that has lower-status characteristics—such as poorer people, those who are nonwhite, and women—is more likely to fear being considered rude for asking questions, and they are more likely to pay serious consequences when they do ask. This is because it is generally considered legitimate to ask only people of equal or lower status than oneself for more information or explanations. It is more likely, then, that lower-status people will be perceived by authorities as "uppity" or ignorant when they behave in these ways. And because of our culture's snobbishness about formal education, people who do not have college or postgraduate degrees tend to fear seeming rude if they ask critical questions of someone who holds a "higher" position than theirs. (They also tend to assume they are too stupid or uneducated to understand or be able to justify a challenge from the authority.)

We cannot let that stop us from asking questions, though, because, as Dr. Jean Hamilton points out,

> A comparison between responses to the two great epidemics of the 80's may be instructive in this regard. That is, the epidemic of HIV-infection and AIDS had been staggering, as had the epidemic of breast cancer. Women clearly had a lot to learn from how gay men and others in the U.S. lobbied for greater public and private funding for AIDS research.[8]

In cases like these, our very lives may be at stake if we don't learn to demand proper treatment—even at the risk of seeming rude or pushy.

- *We think we have no right to think.*

Only certain people are considered legitimate sources of certain kinds of knowledge. In North America, it is generally believed that nutritionists, compared with physicians, have little to teach us about health problems. Trained psychotherapists are thought to know how to solve emotional problems and interpersonal conflicts, but our mothers are often thought to have nothing to contribute. When my house had to be fumigated to flush the squirrels and raccoons out of the space between the inner and outer walls, the exterminators made it clear that they were the experts. They told us we only had to stay away from the house for a few hours after they had done their work. When we returned, I telephoned them to complain, saying that whatever they had used must still be in the house, because my eyes were burning and watering badly. They told me that I didn't know what I was talking about. Did I have an infection? they wondered. They insisted that there was no way that enough chemical could be left to bother me. After ruling out every other possible explanation for my eye trouble, I called them again and requested that their supervisor come to the house. By then I had figured out what must have happened. I asked whether the spray could have been taken into our air-circulation system, and he readily saw that that was possible. At that point, I asked him what spray they had used, and he replied, "Tear gas"—which does hurt the eyes. The mystery had been explained but only after much suffering, and the sole cause for the delay was the experts' belief that, if *they* couldn't explain what was happening to me, then surely I, a layperson, must be mistaken.

Another silencing consequence of the belief that only certain people have the right information about certain topics is that we consumers often hesitate to "ask questions" in the form of seeking untraditional forms of help. We fear that others will think we are silly if we turn, for example, to alternative forms of treatment for physical problems when the medical system has failed to help us. And we fear not only seeming foolish but actually *being* foolish: What if there is no basis for the claims made by people who suggest herbal or vitamin remedies, for instance? It seems to me that we should consider going outside conventional systems when (1) the traditional ones don't seem to be working for us and (2) little or no harm can come from trying other sources. In considering nontraditional methods of doing anything, it may be helpful to know that the National Institutes of Health—which until recently was a bastion of traditionalism—has set up a project for studying alternative methods of healing.

- *We're afraid we'll sound foolish or uninformed.*

The arrogant and territorial attitudes of authorities discussed above convey the message that we are not as smart or knowledgeable as they. Furthermore, we know that we haven't been through medical school, teachers' training, auto mechanics courses, or whatever education the authority in question has had, so we understandably feel uninformed. Often, we're not even sure that we can ask intelligent questions. But laypeople's ability to think logically has been vastly underestimated. Once we get past the jargon and mystification in so many systems, there is little that most of us cannot understand. And if we do ask a question and the expert looks at us as if we are idiots, remember that that undeserved look may be the expert's attempt to silence us. The words of neurologist Oliver Sacks offer some comfort.

> What I found with him [a fellow patient] I found with them all. They were all much wiser than the doctors who treated them! There is among doctors, in acute hospitals at least, a presumption of stupidity, in their patients. And *no one* was "stupid," no one is stupid, except the fools who take them as stupid.[9]

- *If we've never heard anyone else ask the questions that are on our minds, we think that we must be misguided.*

Usually, the public learns that an issue or a procedure is being debated among authorities in a field only if:

1. Each side has a famous, powerful advocate, or
2. A reporter's eye happens to be caught by one of hundreds or thousands of presentations at a conference.

If questions come to our minds that the experts don't seem to have mentioned, we may assume that our questions are unreasonable. But we must remember that having heard nothing about a debate does not mean one isn't going on, for intense debates among experts may rage for years before the public hears about them. And that leads directly to the next inhibitor of consumers' questioning.

- *The media don't encourage critical thinking.*

Maureen Gans and I have described our concern about the lack of journalistic balance in so much reporting:

Journalists who write articles as though scientists were objective do no one any favor. When the material for their story comes from a science journal or from the mouth of someone with an M.D. or a Ph.D., that aura of expertise, those advanced degrees too often cow usually skeptical, hard-boiled reporters into credulity. Reporters and broadcasters commonly assume that, because of the source, the material is indisputably factual, the scholars' or researchers' words are Truth.[10]

A fundamental principle of good journalism is supposed to be interviewing people who have varied and conflicting perspectives on an issue. But it is not uncommon for reporters—who in some ways are deeply skeptical people—to assume that if someone with an M.D. or a Ph.D. after their name claims to have made an important discovery, that person must be speaking the truth, and so there could be no "other side" to explore.

The media vary greatly in the diligence with which they report research. When a researcher recently announced that he had discovered differences between the brains of homosexual and heterosexual men, the *Toronto Star* reporter did not mention an important point that the CNN broadcaster did include: the brains of homosexuals included in the study had come from men who had died from AIDS. It is quite possible that the group differences were due not to their sexual orientations but rather to the fact that one group of brains was riddled with disease, while the other was not.

Science writer Keay Davidson of the *San Francisco Examiner* has described in detail the way that journalists writing about scientific "discoveries" fail to apply critical thinking to their work. He has said that articles about research reports often make dramatic headlines, but when new studies calling those into question are completed, they may not find their way into the newspapers where the original reports appeared.[11] This is particularly true when the original reports are what the public wants or expects to hear, such as "proof" of males' superior intelligence. If the first story made big news, wouldn't you think that a study showing it was wrong would make big news as well? It makes one wonder how editors decide what to print. In spite of the work of some excellent, thoughtful journalists and broadcasters, newspaper articles and broadcast segments too rarely go against what the most powerful people in the various systems and scientific fields believe. As Davidson wrote,

> The press loves studies purporting to prove mental differences between the sexes—and why not? Such studies make great copy. Unfortunately, they can also be used to reinforce the sexist prejudices at the very core of American society. After Sandra Witelson of McMaster University conducted a small, tentative study indicating a different anatomical distinction between the sexes [in one small part of the thin membrane that separates the two halves of the brain from each other]—the *New York Times* couldn't contain its enthusiasm.[12]

Although that study had not been publicly confirmed by any other lab, the *Times* hurried to claim that it could explain a wide range of major differences between the sexes and quoted Witelson as saying that this anatomical difference "is probably just the tip of the iceberg. . . . The anatomy of men's and women's brains may be far more different than we suspect."[13] Davidson warns,

> Whoa, Tex! Suppose a researcher reported discovering a slight anatomical difference between the brains of whites and blacks. Would the *Times* rush into print with a story saying, "This might explain why blacks are so musical and so good at basketball"? And would the researcher have announced: "This anatomical difference is probably just the tip of the iceberg?" Sadly, sexism isn't as "uncool" as racism—even among women.[14]

WHAT CONSUMERS HAVE TO GAIN BY THINKING CRITICALLY

So many powerful forces discourage both authorities and consumers from thinking critically. Understanding the nature and realizing the number of these forces is a major step toward overcoming them and starting to ask more questions. So, too, is realizing what we have to gain from doing so.

As consumers, we need to know that sometimes, the authorities who are most likely to become angry or withhold help because we have questioned them would never have helped us much anyway. But some would have helped, and we have to decide for ourselves when we feel we have little left to lose by breaking our silence. What we gain by speaking up can be better health, greater happiness, and solutions to whatever other problems impelled us to seek help from a system or expert in the first place.

Author Joyce Maynard recently described with a sense of exhilaration the way she got out from under the burden of the common belief that we are destined to repeat our parents' errors. This belief has been vigorously promoted both by many therapists and by the media and has come to be regarded as a truth that applies to *all* people and situations. Maynard writes bravely, flying in the face of popular theory, that her parents made major mistakes in raising her and her sister but that

> I am not doomed to be the victim of my parents' shortcomings and failures. . . . Was I shaped by my dysfunctional origins? Absolutely. The kind of parent I am has everything to do with my experience of growing up in an atmosphere where no such openness existed, and I felt powerless. But [I am] the product of every experience that's come my way.[15]

SOME SUGGESTED STEPS FOR CONSUMERS WHO WANT TO THINK CRITICALLY

As mentioned, there need be nothing mysterious or magical about critical thinking, because it primarily means using common sense and thinking in careful, logical steps. Although some academics have written imposing, jargon-filled books about critical thinking, it should be clear by now that that does *not* mean they are saying anything that cannot be said simply and clearly. So don't be intimidated by what you may hear about "critical thinking." Some of those dearest to me, whom I regard as among the smartest people I know, doubt their own abilities so profoundly that, when they read a term like *critical thinking*, they immediately assume the topic is beyond their reach. They also assume they could never do whatever it might

involve. For that reason, as well as to make sure you understand what I am urging you to do when I exhort you to question the claims and procedures of the experts, I now provide a
smattering of critical thinking techniques. And if you observe
that there is nothing fancy or particularly mystifying about any
of them—that they seem like common sense—you will be
absolutely right. I am not suggesting anything truly novel or
complicated; I simply want you to understand more clearly
how many powerful forces get in the way of your doing these
simple, commonsense things.

Here, then, are some techniques that will help you as the
consumer to think critically or will increase the chances that
authorities with whom you interact will think more carefully
and critically about what they are doing. But as you put these
suggestions to use, remember that I include each one because
it has worked in at least some if not all instances. Above all,
remember that if you try them and they are not effective, *that
does not mean that you didn't do them well enough.*

—*If you feel as though you have no right to question the
experts, as though you need their permission to do so, ask yourself, "Why do I feel this way? Do I feel that it is morally right to
grant them (or for them to have) the power to make me feel this
way? Would I want them to wield such power over my best friend
or my loved ones?"* Sometimes, just asking yourself such questions can make you feel less afraid and help you identify what
is getting in the way of your holding the experts accountable or
inquiring about what they say and do.

—*Before you have your next appointment with or write your
next letter to the authority, make a list of questions that you
would like to have answered,* such as "What are all of the different ways this problem could be handled, and what are the pros
and cons of each? What are the chances that each of these
ways could really be implemented—for instance, that *your*
supervisor would agree to each one?" Writing such questions
will help ensure that your mind doesn't go blank when you confront the power and jargon of the expert. Knowing you have
this list, the experts will be more likely to assume that you have
thought about the issues and have some knowledge of them,

and some will be more responsive and cooperative as a result. Making such a list will also reduce the chances that your conversation will be deflected into less important or irrelevant areas, because you can periodically glance at your list and keep the discussion on track. If it veers off, you can remind the expert that you still have three questions left for which you would like to have responses. The list will also help both you and the expert to gauge your time and try to distribute it sensibly, in view of the number of questions you have.

—*At the beginning of your conversation or letter, tell the authority how many questions you would like to have answered.* If you are in a face-to-face meeting or a telephone conversation, *ask how much time the authority has set aside for the meeting.* If it seems to you that will not be enough time to answer all your questions, ask if you can take as much time as you need or when you can make an appointment to finish the questions. Confirming at the beginning of a conversation how much time has been set aside may be helpful in a couple of ways. First, it gives you some control over how much time is spent on each topic. It is frustrating to spend time on one question because you feel you are really getting somewhere, only to have the authority say, "Well, time is up!" when your other questions are still unasked. Second, when you have just read a list of five clearly important questions, authorities who really want to help may be less likely to say, "We have only six minutes for this meeting." Having to say that can jolt some authorities into awareness of how unreasonable their time constraints are and may make them more inclined to set aside additional time for you.

—*Try to begin by asking a question that you know the authority may be willing to answer and may feel good about,* such as, "Has the medicine reduced my mother's fever today, doctor?" In this way, you decrease somewhat the likelihood that the authority will become immediately defensive. If you feel infuriated at the idea of having to stroke the authority's ego to increase the chances of getting the information or help you want, you will have to choose whether to drop this suggestion or to implement it anyway because the alternatives are limited or nonexistent. But there is, in fact, an important difference between stroking someone's ego (out of fear or unjustified respect) and trying to set a pleasant, cooperative tone that might lead to a more favorable outcome for you and that simply feels more human. When I tried to get the workers to fix the front steps that they had installed incorrectly at my house, I began the conversation by telling them how lovely the steps looked (fighting off the mild nausea I felt at saying this) before then saying that they were collecting great pools of water.

—*As the authority speaks, take very careful notes.* This can increase both the authority's critical thinking and your own. Many experts are more responsible and careful about what they say when their words are written down—or tape-recorded (though the latter can backfire and make some of them extremely defensive and uncooperative); your taking notes reminds them that, at least on a moral level, they are accountable to you. And either *while* you are writing or *after* the conversation, the simple act of noting what the authority says can help you spot any lapses in logic or failure to answer your questions or address your concerns; the authority's manipulative *ways* of talking or nonverbal signals that tell you "You should agree to everything I am saying" are less effective when you are writing. A friend whose dentist recently told her she needed an enormous number of dental procedures, as well as an expensive new toothbrush and more frequent, regular checkups, felt overwhelmed and confused. As the dentist tried to rush her out of his office, she said calmly, "Now, I want to make sure I understand all of this, so let me just write it down. You said, for instance, that I need to buy a $110.00 electric toothbrush. What are the reasons for that? And how much more effective has that been proven to be than a regular one?" Had the dentist refused to answer each of her questions, she would have questioned the validity of his advice and sought another opinion. But as he answered each question, she felt less overwhelmed and in a better position to assess which steps seemed crucial to her dental care and which were desirable but not urgent. In fact, she asked him to specify, "Which of these recommendations do you consider essential, which ones desirable but not urgent, and which ones just a little bit helpful?"

—When experts use jargon or say anything you do not under-stand, continue to take notes and ask, "Would you please explain that in words that I can understand?" If they resist explaining clearly, you might try saying, "I want to be sure that I can explain this to my [child, father, employer, etc.], so I need for you to say it in a simpler way."

—Ask for brochures or articles that you can take away with you, so that you can think critically about the issues when you are on your own or with friends or family.

—Whenever you feel pressed by the expert to make a decision or agree to anything, consider asking for time to think about it. That may not be possible in an emergency, but sometimes even tak-ing a couple of minutes to think—alone or with others—*outside* of the expert's presence and power can give you the mental and emotional space you need to think clearly.

—Tell friends and family members what the authorities are saying to you, and have a brainstorming session with them aimed at identifying which questions you need to ask and which ones you have asked but for which you have not received satisfac-tory answers. This can be extremely helpful because it is easier to apply an inquiring approach when you are not *at that moment* in the presence of an authority who is intimidating you, intentionally or not.

—When you recount your interactions with authorities to your family and friends, ask them if they hear signs that the authori-ties are biased. Does the plumber, for instance, seem to be push-ing you toward replumbing your entire house, without having convinced you that this is absolutely unavoidable? Does your therapist seem intent on getting you to blame your mother for all your problems, even though you feel you have a good rela-tionship with her?

—Check with friends, other people who have been through the same system, and librarians about the full range of your options. For instance, if you have gotten poor results from a high-priced lawyer, explore what one of the lower-priced ones has to offer. Or if you have physical symptoms that medical doctors have not been able to alleviate, investigate less traditional alterna-tives. An example of the latter is the practice of Tai Chi move-

ments by people who have Parkinson's disease. Although this is certainly a nontraditional "treatment," apparently there is now even medical evidence that

> the improved [blood] circulation which results from practicing Tai Chi is seen as promoting drug absorption [of the drugs used to treat the disease] and minimizing toxic side effects. In addition, some doctors have begun to realize that many of the negative changes associated with Parkinson's are partly a result of decreased physical activity rather than the disease itself.[16]

—Identify a claim or a piece of advice the authority has given you, and ask yourself, "If I were in that authority's position, what would have to be true for me to make that claim or give that advice?" For instance, if the doctor says, "We really must use a general anesthetic when we operate on your father," ask yourself, "If I were this doctor, what would I have to know before making a statement like that? I would have to know that with only a local anesthetic, the patient would hear the sound of the saw on his leg bone, and that would probably be very disconcerting. Or I would have to know that the surgery will be extremely long and that this patient would probably become highly agitated by having to endure such an extended procedure while awake. Or I would have to know that, in view of this patient's age and physical condition, there are only minimal risks from a general, as opposed to a local, anesthetic." Because you are not the authority in this case, you are less likely to have a particular approach to defend and are more likely to be concerned about the patient. This frees you to think about what questions you will want the doctor to consider before you and your father agree to the recommended course of action. Then you can ask the doctor about those various issues, find out what assumptions she is making about your father—and on what basis she makes those assumptions (for instance, you might know that he is actually very calm in the face of danger or stress), and *ask her where you can read up about the information behind her recommendations.* Making such a query will tend to render the expert less apt to make thoughtless, unsubstantiated statements.

—*If you yourself need help from the system, always ask yourself, "If my parent or child or best friend were being dealt with in this way, would I consider it unfair or biased or cavalier? In what way? Is the authority simply acting too rushed to give me a full explanation of what is happening, and would I be furious if he treated someone I care about in that way? Would I consider his behavior, if directed at someone else, to be racist, ageist, sexist, and the like?"* This is a crucial exercise, because, as noted, most people find it easier to see when others are being improperly or unfairly treated than when they themselves are.

—*Watch for the blatantly false statement.* When I was studying the research on sex differences in spatial abilities and read an "expert's" claim that the lack of women chess champions helped prove that females were inferior, that so startled me that it led me to question his other, more complex claims as well.

—*If the authority with whom you are currently dealing is not helping you or is seriously upsetting you, think about who might be more willing to help.* Sometimes this means a lateral move, such as going to another doctor for a second opinion. At other times, this means going straight to the top, because those at the top often have more power to help you and have fewer people over their heads who might disapprove if they do something unorthodox. When I was a junior at Radcliffe College, the heat went off in our dormitory in the dead of winter. Many of us telephoned the buildings and grounds office to complain, and then we spent several hours freezing, our hands and feet stuffed into the hats of, our portable, 1960s-style hair dryers for warmth. As we got progressively colder, I followed the precept taught me by my maternal grandmother, Esther Milner Karchmer, and my mother, Tac Karchmer Caplan, and went straight to the top. I telephoned the office of the president of the college and asked to speak with her. I was told she was busy and was asked what I wanted. I informed the secretary that I suspected that the president might not be aware that the heat was off in Daniels Hall, and I felt sure she would not be wanting us to freeze. Within the hour, the heat was fixed, and of course I shall never know whether or not my phone call made the difference. But such contacts can be very effective.

—*Don't worry about the authorities' thinking you are pushy or impolite or simply not very nice for asking questions.* Remember that the point is not to convince them you are nice and compliant but to get the information or action you need. Although it is a good idea to begin by being nice and as patient as the situation warrants (if your child is in the emergency room, there may be little time for good manners), don't let them make you feel your job is to remain that way if the needed service is not forthcoming. Remember, too, that when most of us need help and are not getting it, we are naturally upset. The contrast between how emotional we feel, on the one hand, and the authority's likely calm, inexpressive demeanor, on the other, can make us feel as though we are foolish or overly emotional. And this can inhibit us from asking questions. But being aware of this factor can help us recognize when we are feeling that way, set that feeling aside, and go ahead and ask our questions anyway.

—*When you are feeling too intimidated to ask questions or push or answers, pretend (in your own mind) that you are someone else.* I have often pretended to be my mother or my grandmother in such situations. And when I am feeling frantic but need to behave as though I feel calm and in control, I pretend I am a friend of mine who always looks calm and in control. I am delighted to find how well this often works for me.

Although I cannot promise miracles, such simple, critical thinking steps sometimes lead to wonderful outcomes. In the following two excerpts, for instance, two different people who used the technique of turning to someone higher up or just to someone different in the system got very positive results:

> [For over ten years, a man had reported symptoms that his doctor said were due to other problems.] One day while waiting at an airport, his wife saw a man from behind who was slumped over and shuffling along. She thought, 'That man is ill.' When he turned around, she was shocked—the man was her husband! A visit to another doctor resulted in a quick diagnosis of Parkinson's. A new perspective had been needed. . . .
> . . . [In another case,] In the waiting room of Dr. Feldman's office, Blaine and I met an elderly patient whose walk and

speech were close to normal. [He] had been confined to a wheel chair, had spoken only in a mumble, and had been very weak (a typical Parkinsonian in the latter stages of the disease) as recently as only one year earlier! Now, under the care of Dr. Feldman, he was in for a check-up before he drove alone to Florida, where he would spend the winter months! Having evaluated his first doctor, he had changed doctors and treatment, and was certainly enjoying the results.[17]

The suggestions in this chapter should help you start thinking critically about your experiences within various institutions. And virtually all of the suggestions in Chapter 8, of strategies for dealing with your feelings of stupidity and powerlessness, involve some form of critical thinking as well.

8

Reacting and Resisting, Saving Your Sanity

What You Can Do

This chapter is about some strategies I have learned—from others or through my own experience—that can be helpful when we feel stupid and powerless in the face of a daunting system or expert. The strategies are aimed at decreasing those feelings of being stupid, powerless, and culpable.

The particular suggestions in this chapter that any one of you will find helpful will vary as much as your personalities. I suggest you look first for suggestions that feel the most comfortable for you, those you think you could carry out with little or no effort. But also consider them again to see which ones might never have occurred to you. Sometimes, you can be pleasantly surprised by the results of trying strategies you believed to be beyond your repertoire—or that simply never came to mind. It is essential to be aware that not every one of these strategies will be useful, or even possible, in every situation, so screen the suggestions with that in mind. And remember that no matter what you do, sometimes the system will not help or serve you, and realize that that is not your fault.

Being under the pressure of struggling with an unhelpful system whose assistance we need can so drain our energies and demand our attention that we cannot think of much we could do. Psychologist Nikki Gerrard points out the difference between "choosing" and "coping"[1]: When our lives are going along smoothly, we are relatively free to *choose* how to act, but when we are mistreated or oppressed, we are limited to *coping* because we have less energy and fewer options. When we encounter rigid, ungiving systems at a time of need, our energy is already depleted, and few of us have the luxury of devoting ourselves full-time to making the systems work as they should. Furthermore, the very nature and power of many systems and authorities limits our options: The judicial system and the Workers' Compensation structures are unlikely to change much in response to our individual entreaties, and distant experts who issue pronouncements about how to raise our children or save our marriages needn't even respond to our reports that their recommendations didn't work for us.

Recognizing the limits of what you can do on your own and right away should not be demoralizing, for you may be able to bring about more changes if you work in concert with others and over long periods of time. But this book is primarily intended to help you hoard your strength and self-esteem in the short term, so that you can deal with your current crisis with a minimum of harm to yourself and those you love. Once you have gotten through that crisis, you may well choose longer-term, group efforts aimed at modifying institutions or changing individual authorities' behavior so that others will not have to suffer as you have.

Remember, then, that the strategies are aimed first and foremost at helping you to see the situation clearly, to reduce unjustified self-blame and feelings of stupidity and inadequacy. Not letting the system exhaust or destroy you is certainly a kind of victory. Although these strategies will not necessarily help you get the system or expert to do what you want, in some circumstances they may have those effects. Keep in mind, as discussed in Chapter 4, that some of the people in these systems do care about you, and if, for instance, you point out which techniques they are using, they may try to change their behavior in ways that will ultimately benefit you. As you read these suggestions, you may again wonder whether I take a completely gloomy view of authorities. Let me say again that I do not. But you don't need coping strategies for dealing with those authorities who are helpful. The whole purpose of this chapter is to offer strategies for when you encounter those who do not, or will not, help and who leave you feeling stupid and powerless.

Now here are some specific suggestions for coping.

UNDERSTAND

—Understand that much of what we (or our taxes) are paying the authorities or experts to do is to give us information.

—Understand that evidence or data *can* often be used to argue more than one side of an issue. For instance, researchers who claim that because some (usually poorly conducted) research has shown that some women do not function as well just before their menstrual periods as at other times of the month, no women should be allowed to fly airplanes. However, one might well argue that, because it is easy for some women to know when their periods are due and, if they feel bad at those times, to avoid flying then, with men we don't have such an easy way of predicting poor performance, and so we should never let any men fly planes. So follow the Rival Hypothesis Principle[2]: When you hear a claim about what is right or true, search carefully and long for other possible explanations of the available information. If your physician tells you that the only thing you can do about the large number of colds you get every year is to take antihistamines and decongestants, you might (1) ask yourself, other physicians, and alternative healthcare workers whether an underlying problem (such as a weakened immune system) might need to be understood and addressed, rather than simply treating the symptoms each time they develop; and (2) ask other physicians, alternative healthcare workers, and friends, and seek out reading materials for suggestions for other treatments that might work (such as the fenugreek Arnie used to get rid of his long-term cough).

—Understand that the experts themselves may hate the charade that they can really help you. Sometimes just keeping that in mind can minimize the damage to you. Elaine, who had applied for Workers' Compensation because the building in which she worked made her ill, was quite frustrated when her request for compensation was refused. She telephoned the Workers' Compensation worker who had been in charge of her case and said, "I am upset that my claim was denied, but I realize that you were in a difficult position, since sick building syndrome is only beginning to be recognized as harmful to people's health, so there probably wasn't much that you could do. I guess that it would have been easier if the physicians on your staff had been more enlightened about this kind of problem and that, without their support, your hands were pretty much tied." Saying that did nothing to change the decision about her claim, but Elaine felt a little bit better for having named the reality of what had happened and for having reached through the bureaucracy to make some brief, human contact with the worker, whose hands were indeed tied.

—Understand that some experts think you will lose respect for them if they don't have all the answers. So give the expert a chance to say, "I just don't know." You may want to remark that you realize not everything is understood in this field and you wonder whether that applies to your case. One of my greatest moments of truth came when I told the parents of a three-year-old child I had been asked to assess that I simply didn't know what was wrong with him. I knew that he wasn't autistic or retarded and didn't appear schizophrenic, but he did indeed seem strange; however, I said, I had never seen or read about his particular combination of characteristics and behavior. I didn't know what to predict, but I urged the parents to use their own judgment about their child's needs, and I offered to see the child again in six months or at the parents' request. The parents heaved a great sigh of relief and said that, after having carted their son to five different professionals, each of whom tossed various labels at them but left them feeling confused, they had begun to suspect that no one really knew what was wrong with their child. That bothered them less than trying to find out from the experts *whether* anything could be done. With the first five, they had had to spend most of their time being the targets of professional-sounding gobbledygook that included no practical suggestions but left the parents feeling it was their own fault to have been unable to grasp what they were being told.

—Understand the likely motives behind their jargon and their name-calling (Chapter 4).

—Understand that when they blame you or call you names, whatever their motives, they are trying to make their job easier by silencing you and making you more pliant and submissive.

—Understand that, when dealing with some authorities, you are damned either way: If you don't object to the way you are treated, you will remain mystified, uninformed, and powerless. If you question or challenge the experts, they may become more helpful, but they also may accuse you of being paranoid, unreasonable, and demanding, and you or others close to you could suffer reprisals (for instance, a challenged principal may place your child with a terrible teacher). When you go up against the system, it doesn't pay to be naive about what is at stake, but once you see that the alternative is to continue in your current, frustrated state, the choice may feel easier. And at least you will be making an informed decision.

Depending upon the degree of goodwill and, possibly, the authority's position in the system's hierarchy, you may or may not be able to do anything to avoid being called paranoid. When authorities have little or no stake in helping you, they simply must find ways to dismiss your legitimate questions in order to protect themselves and avoid providing appropriate services. However, it is worth starting by assuming they do wish to help, because some of them do, in which case the principles of "expressive training" will enable you to ask your questions and express your concerns in a way that maximizes the chances you will be heard and responded to.[3] (If this doesn't work, you can, of course, try other strategies.) The key principles are as follows:

1. Do not make threats, demands, or criticisms. This means no name-calling and no phrases such as "If you don't do this, I'll . . ." or "You don't really care about my child!"
2. State clearly and simply what you feel and why. For instance, instead of saying, "I don't know why you haven't answered our questions," try saying, "We would like for you to explain, in terms that we can understand, every one of the treatment possibilities for Aunt Ernestine and all of the possible side effects of each treatment. Or if there are some clearly written pamphlets or articles containing that information, perhaps you could direct us to those."

—Understand that the effect of jargon is to mystify you. If you don't comprehend what the experts are saying, do not assume that that is *your* failing. Among themselves, experts may believe they use jargon to save time, but when they use technical language or linguistic shortcuts with clients, it is often at the expense of the clients' understanding. A community psychologist who works exclusively with farmers and their families told me that many of them are hopelessly mystified by bankers' and lawyers' language. As a result, when they receive a notice of foreclosure, they simply pack up and leave, because they cannot imagine how they might talk to the banker about what the foreclosure notice really means, whether or not it means the farmer has to vacate the property, or how they should go about breaking through the technical language in their notices.

—Understand that even experienced professionals can make horrendous mistakes. A friend of mine with a history of high blood pressure was taking medication to lower it. Then he was diagnosed with cancer, and while initially hospitalized for surgery, he was placed on painkilling medication as well. When he was sent home, he frequently complained of pain and great fatigue and asked for more painkillers, which the doctor had told him he could take as needed. His wife and sisters urged him to "take a more positive attitude and stop complaining so much." They told him he couldn't expect to feel good so soon after surgery. Weeks later, when it was time to renew his prescriptions, his wife discovered that when they had first been filled, the pharmacist had accidentally switched the labels. Thus, the poor man had been unknowingly overdosing on his blood pressure medication, thinking it was the drug for pain, so that his pain had not been relieved, and he had also suffered the side effects of too many blood-pressure pills.

ASSUME

—Assume community. Even if you have to begin doing this as an act of faith, assume that there are other people in the same boat as you, feeling the same frustration and humiliation. In my own experience, this has never turned out to be a wrong assumption, and once you make it, it strengthens you: You don't feel so weird or alone, even if you don't yet know exactly who else is being treated this way. It becomes easier to talk to others about your dilemma, and invariably you discover kindred spirits.

A woman who believed she was being subtly mistreated by her lawyer because of her race—but feared perhaps she was actually paranoid instead—brought up the subject at a church group meeting. She began by describing what had happened as though the victim had been "a close friend," because she suspected she was the only person who had ever had such experiences. As soon as she told the first story, however, she saw a few of her listeners nodding as they connected it with what had happened to them. Eventually, she acknowledged that these were her own stories and said she thought they were signs of her lawyer's racist attitudes. She was gratified to find that many of her friends shared her view.

A good indication that those who work in institutions are trying to prevent you from recognizing that community is the phrase, "You're the only one who ever . . . [complained, asked for this, etc.]." Sometimes, those with authority will try to draw you into a sense of community with *them* rather than with those they are mistreating in the same way. In Chapter 2, I described my faculty's unwillingness, when I was in graduate school, to let me attend two psychotherapy case conferences rather than the usual one. They had expressed concern that, if they did it for me, they would have to do it for everyone. They were attempting to draw me into a sense of community with them rather than with the other students, asking me to share their fear that this would open imagined floodgates to such requests. It is crucial in such cases to ask ourselves where our true community lies. In the above instance, I asked myself, "If other students *did* make the same request, and the faculty had to honor it, would that be bad for the students?" The answer, of course, was no. In fact, it wouldn't even have required any more work from the faculty, because students were not required to hand in assignments that professors would have to read and mark for that course. When you hear such phrases as "If we did it for you, we would have to do it for everyone," it is also helpful to ask yourself whether it is very likely that similar requests would pour forth. In my case, when I persisted, I was allowed to attend the two case conferences, yet not a single other student asked to do so. They were plenty busy without having to attend additional classes.

Neurologist Oliver Sacks illustrates from his own experience the devastating effects of the *absence* of a sense of community. When Sacks's leg was injured in an accident, he told his doctor that he was unable to contract some of his thigh muscles and could not tell where his leg was positioned except by looking at it. Sacks writes:

> I had a feeling that Swan [the physician] looked frightened for a moment, but it was so momentary, so fugitive, that I could not be sure.
>
> "Nonsense, Sacks," he said sharply and decisively. "There's nothing the matter. Nothing at all. Nothing to be worried about. Nothing at all!"
>
> "But . . . "
>
> "He held up his hand, like a policeman halting traffic. "You're completely mistaken," he said with finality. "There's nothing wrong with the leg. You understand that, don't you?"[4]

Years later, tests showed there had been and still was quite severe nerve damage that caused the symptoms Sacks's physician had denied. Sacks writes that all of his upsetting feelings would have been

> tolerable, or more tolerable, if [they] could be communicated to others, and become a subject of understanding and sympathy— like grief. This was denied me when the surgeon said "Nothing," so that I was thrown into the further hell—the hell of communication denied. [And this] so contradicted and questioned and doubted my (most elemental) perceptions—perceptions on which my most elemental sense of "I," self-integrity, was based.[5]

—Assume that you know a great deal. Assume you are as smart and as capable of understanding as the "experts." Making notes, perhaps in a journal, and reading them over can be immensely helpful in feeling sure about what you know. Leah met weekly with a social worker who was acting as a mediator in Leah's divorce. The social worker said one thing on a Tuesday, and that went into Leah's journal. The following Tuesday, Leah thought she was going crazy, because she could have sworn the mediator was now totally reversing what she had said the week before. However, at this emotionally burdensome time in her life and in the face of the mediator's self-assured demeanor, Leah blamed herself for having misunderstood the week before. Fortunately, she checked her journal entry from the previous week as soon as she returned home and found that she was not the confused one.

Even when journal keeping doesn't work, starting from the simple assumption that you are reasonably intelligent can be very useful. A widower came to me in a state of confusion, because his son's teacher had said the child had "an intractable, acting-out behavior disorder" and the father should "do something" about it. The father had felt intimidated because the teacher seemed to feel his son's behavior was his fault and had presented her concerns in an angry, accusatory way. This had so thrown him that he had escaped from the interview at the earliest possible moment. Only after he got home did he realize he had no idea what the teacher meant by "intractable, acting-out behavior disorder." It sounded bad, and that increased his anxiety even more, so that he was having a very difficult time even thinking about the content of what she had said.

I suggested that, instead of assuming he couldn't understand her technical language because he had only a ninth-grade education, he try to calm down so we could think clearly about what the teacher had said. I asked him to assume instead that, once he could relax a bit, he would be able to understand what she had told him and that, if he could not, it was due not to his own limitations but to her failure to make her meaning clear. When he calmed down, he took out a dictionary, looked up "intractable," and found that it meant his son's problem was impossible to deal with. He knew right away that this wasn't true, because he himself had found ways of bringing his son's occasionally destructive behavior under control. He couldn't find "acting-out" or "behavior disorder" in the dictionary, so I told him that the first term was jargon for "shows his distress by behaving in disruptive or problematic ways, rather than by, for instance, withdrawing," and the second term meant that there was something wrong with his son's entire personality and that it was probably unchangeable. Again, because of his direct experience with his son, the father realized that the second term did not apply, for the child functioned perfectly well in most places most of the time. He also realized that "acting out" was an accurate description of his child's behavior. Understanding the meanings of these terms, he knew that it was not that the teacher was so much smarter than he but rather that she used more complicated (and partly inaccurate) terms than necessary. It was important for this man to know that his imagined lack of intelligence was unjustified.

The above example echoes one of the suggestions for doing critical thinking mentioned in Chapter 7: to take careful notes about what authorities tell you. Once you have recorded what they say, you are in a position to check out the meanings of their terms or the implications of their claims by your own research (if there's time) in libraries, with friends, with people who work in the system in question, and so on.

Educator Debby Storch once made the kind of remark that seems simple and obvious once we have heard it but too rarely occurs to most of us. Commenting on how frequently most laypeople assume they know far less than they actually do know, she observed that many parents worry desperately that they are not "providing enough early intellectual stimulation for their babies and toddlers." They rush to bookstores and prominent educators, begging for books and kits that will show them how to increase their children's intelligence. However, Storch pointed out, "Many immigrant parents didn't do 'early intellectual stimulation' with their children, but they raised many extremely accomplished, intelligent, and successful off-spring."[6] In the face of powerful systems, such basic, simple principles can become lost. We begin to doubt the value of our own common sense and the truth of our direct observations. Assuming community and similarity helps us resist such self-doubt and reclaim the right to speak up and out as something that good citizens, rather than "troublemakers," do.

LEARN

—Learn as much as you can about the subject before you see the experts. But remember, although it is a great idea to ask for assistance at the public library in finding information about your situation and the system with which you are dealing, or to ask others within the system for information, in some circumstances you are unavoidably limited because of time pressures or the unavailability of resources. For example, if you need emergency surgery, you haven't the luxury of doing extensive library research; then, too, some systems are better than others about disclosing information about their work and procedures. Keep in mind, too, that no matter how well informed you are, the degrees of the authority's goodwill *and* power within the system will be major determinants of the outcome of your search for help.

—Learn that anger is a secondary emotion. Human beings don't go from feeling nothing to feeling angry. First, you have a feeling you don't like having—such as shame or powerless-ness—and then you get angry about having that feeling. Although sometimes venting your anger at persons in authority can make them sit up, take notice, and help you, often it only makes them shut down, close you out altogether, or even before more punitively. For your own sake, it is helpful to use anger as a signal that something is wrong. So when you feel angry, try to identify what is causing that anger. Once you realize, "That guy makes me feel foolish, because he keeps telling me that I need a letter from my CR in order to get into the HC—but I don't know what CR and HC stand for," it's a simple matter to ask him to explain the abbreviations. In more complex situations, once I realize my anger comes from feeling totally ineffective, if the expert won't listen to what I have to say, I *can* figure out what else I can do to feel—and perhaps to become—more powerful. This may mean going over the fellow's head to his supervisor, forming a self-help group, or alerting the media to what is going on.

—Learn to make the translations. For instance, if they are calling you a troublemaker, it is usually appropriate for you to translate that—every time you think or speak about it—into "I am not a trouble*maker*. Rather, I have *called attention to existing trouble*." When experts tell you you're an ungrateful wretch for asking how they made their decisions, in your mind immediately translate "ungrateful wretch" into "informed and active consumer." Go even farther: Cast yourself (if only in the silence of your own mind) as a pilgrim, a pioneer, one of A Few Brave Souls. This can give you strength and help you remember, when accused of being ungrateful, obnoxious, or destructive, that your aim is to empower yourself (and, hopefully, others) and to do a bit to humanize the system in which you are struggling to operate and to survive.

ASK

—Always ask for more information. Even when you think you may have been told everything, ask if there is further information available—from brochures, public documents, other clients/consumers. Asking for more does not guarantee, of course, that you will learn all there is to know. But it makes it somewhat more likely that you will get more of the information you need. That information may consist of practical details that will help you decide what to do, or it may consist of information that makes you feel less crazy. For instance, a woman filed a complaint about the unethical way a lawyer had dealt with her. This set in motion a prolonged process during which her complaint was declared valid and the lawyer was censured. Months later, however, after no further contact with her, a representative of the bar association wrote to her, saying that the lawyer had phoned the representative to say that her allegations were untrue, and so the representative had reversed her previous decision. Appalled by the injustice and impropriety of this reversal—all the more because the legal system is supposed to be based on fair hearing—she had nowhere to turn. One after another, members of the bar association staff told her that there was no route of appeal. No one volunteered the opinion that she had been shabbily and unfairly treated. She continued to contact association members higher and higher in the hierarchy, and at last from one of their top people she heard the words, "Well, you know, that reversal without even giving you a chance to reply was totally unprecedented, and it never should have happened." The bar association never did correct their grievous error, but the complainant did feel certain that her indignation and anger had *not* been overreactions.

—Ask yourself (and others) if there are inconsistencies in what the authority says or contradictions in what different authorities say. For instance, does your pediatrician tell you to trust your parental instincts in dealing with your child's health but berate you for not bringing the child to the emergency room when she had a fever of two degrees above normal?

—Ask yourself: What reason does this person or institution have to try to do its very best *for me*? This can be especially helpful in switching us away from believing that ungiving people and institutions are really trying to help us, so that if we are not *feeling* helped, it must be our own fault. It can rapidly remind us that experts and workers in institutions often have their own agendas, needs, and pressures that have nothing to do with serving us.

Related to asking yourself what reason the authority would

have to treat you well is asking yourself what might be the motives of the authority for treating you badly. As Atwood writes,

> Be sure to question the motives of a doctor who gets irritated if you ask questions or if you want a second opinion. If a doctor is more motivated by his own insecurities than he is by your need for the best treatment, you may want to find another doctor. Remember, if your illness remains poorly diagnosed or poorly treated, *you* are the one who will suffer, not the doctor.[7]

—Ask one or more friends to go with you for appointments with experts. Many of us find it easier to see that our friends are intelligent than to acknowledge our own good sense. And many of us can see more clearly when an expert gives someone else the runaround than when it is given to us. A mother took her young daughter to a social worker specializing in incest after the daughter said her father had been "touching me inside" and pointed to her vulva. The social worker, in the mother's presence, made a videotape of the child telling him the same story. But after the socialworker confronted the father with the accusation, and the father categorically denied having abused his daughter, the worker began chiding the mother for having made up the story. He claimed that the child had never really said anything that suggested her father had sexually abused her; furthermore, he doubted she even knew where her vulva was. Wondering if she was going crazy or losing her memory, the mother asked a friend to go with her to view the videotape in the social worker presence, and she was greatly relieved when her friend confirmed her impressions. When we are under great stress, it is easy to doubt our own perceptions and recollections, because we suspect that the stress might have interfered with our thinking and memory.

—Ask to speak to someone else, preferably someone with more authority or power, and say why you are making that request. Atwood describes the encouraging results of Faylene's insistence on consulting another doctor after she suffered severe side effects from the high dosage of medication her local doctor had prescribed for her Parkinson's disease. While trying to work, she struggled with "uncontrollable involuntary move-ments, slurred speech, and the fear that her supervisor would stop by and see her at her worst. . . . She was embarrassed because her condition made her seem drunk."[8] After six months of this, her local doctor hospitalized her for observation but sent her home with all the same problems. At last, she sought a different doctor, who discovered that one-ninth her former dose controlled her Parkinson's symptoms adequately and did not cause the negative side effects.

—Ask yourself, Would they treat a man, a white person, a wealthier person, a more educated person, their co-worker, their boss this way? While the real answer may be that they might do so, there might be certain things they would not have dared to do to them that they freely do to you. This is another strategy that can suddenly and radically shift our perspective away from self-blame, because it reminds us that people with power are more likely to mistreat those they see as vulnerable or inferior to themselves than those they see as nearer their own level.

BEWARE

—Beware of victim blame. When the expert starts blaming you (or your child, or whoever the client may be) for the problem, realize that that is probably unprofessional behavior and prob-ably also just plain wrong.

—Beware of the tendency of those who work in major insti-tutions to regard and treat you as though you are totally differ-ent from them, as though you come from another species, as though you are not fully human.

—Beware of allowing anyone to convince you that to ques-tion or to challenge is disrespectful, nasty, or even un-Ameri-can. Isn't a questioning, open attitude exactly what we hope to learn in our schooling and to teach to the next generation? The fact that the particular questions we are asking at any given time make someone uncomfortable does *not* indicate that we are wrong for asking. It may be helpful to recall that a child who accidentally knocks over a lamp will become uncomfortable and resentful if you ask, "Did you do that?" As noted earlier in this chapter, there are ways to increase the chances that your questions or challenges will be heard and responded to helpfully, but so much depends on the integrity of the authority's motives. The primary aim of some authorities is to defend the system or their own actions; for them, the very fact that you don't silently accept their instructions and slink away will unavoidably threaten them—and many people cope with feeling threatened by accusing and attacking the source of that feeling.

—Beware of information that those who work for institutions will not feel they need to reveal to you, especially when their silence protects their institution. As we have seen, major systems and experts will go to great lengths to cover up any evidence that they do harm. Pilisuk writes,

> Responsibility for discovery [of problems] lies with the survivor, not with the purveyor of the offending technology or with society at large. Often the technological consequence is subtle: an increase in tiredness, an allergic reaction, proneness to infection. Sometimes (as with the veterans of atomic testing) there are no symptoms until years after an exposure that went unnoticed at the time.[9]

In some cases, those in institutions may genuinely not know that their system has caused harm, but in other cases they know and actively work to cover it up. None of us *likes* to be suspicious, but sometimes it is realistic and self-protective to consider the possibility of a cover-up.

EXIT

—Exit from their framework, even if you cannot leave their system. When you are involved in a particular system, it is so easy to start sharing its assumptions and values, even without realizing it. The major purpose of Chapters 2 through 7 is to make it easier to recognize that the authorities do not always defend and stand for Truth, Justice, and the American Way but that they are human, subjective, biased, and filled with needs and fears of their own, and that they work within systems that make it likely they will resort to one or more of the stupefying and disempowering techniques. What can help you exit from their framework is scanning the list of techniques that follows Chapter 1, as well as rereading some of the examples in Chapters 2 and 3 to help you identify and keep vividly in mind which techniques are being used to your detriment.

Getting out of the framework can mean learning to make the necessary translations (for instance, from "trouble*maker*" to "one who sees where the trouble lies"; see also the Learn section, above).

Getting out of the framework can also mean learning to trust your own perceptions. If a Workers' Compensation interviewer smiles and chats with you every time you meet, but you realize every time you leave that she has given you no concrete help at all, do not feel you must believe that she is helping you. Instead, think of your interactions as, "She acts friendly but gives me no help."

—Consider just leaving the system *or* ceasing all contact with the expert who is making you feel stupid and powerless. If it becomes completely clear to you that you will not get the help you are seeking, that the suffering you are enduring outweighs the benefits you just *might* obtain *someday*, or that *for now* the suffering is too great, then consider whether it might be possible to use your energy and time more effectively. For instance, a couple who believed that their school board was neglecting their son's need for special help in reading forfeited many days' wages as they skipped work to have endless meetings with unresponsive school employees. As it became clear to them that those designated by the school to help such children had no intention of assigning their child to a special-help category, they began to look at two different possibilities: (1) not skipping work anymore but instead using some of their wages to hire a private tutor for their child and (2) describing their frustrating experiences in a letter to their local, elected school board officials.

ACT

—When you are receiving unsatisfactory service from authorities, write down their names and ask for the names of their supervisors and the directors or heads of the institutions. Sometimes, just that is enough to encourage the person with whom you are dealing to be more helpful. But you may need to write a letter to that person's supervisor and, ultimately, to the person at the top, detailing your concerns and your dissatisfaction and stating clearly what service you are seeking. If you write such a letter, the notes you have been keeping throughout your involvement in that system will be extremely useful in allowing you to document the exact timing of the problems and delays, as well as the precise details of what has happened.

—After any meeting or telephone conversation you have with any authority, consider sending a follow-up memo, in which you note the important points about who said what, what the authority promised to do or to find out, and what you have or have not agreed to.

—In person or in writing, name and describe to the authority with whom you are dealing those techniques that they have been using to make you feel stupid and powerless. Sometimes, simply naming what is going on is surprisingly effective, either because the perpetrators of the technique depend upon your silent acquiescence to carry it off or because they haven't realized what they are doing in such stark terms as "I am fragmenting this person I am supposed to be helping."

Mary Jo used this strategy with an authority who was using Technique 9, claiming that what she wanted him to do was not his responsibility. The telephone company had threatened to cut off her service because she had not paid a gigantic bill. She had made six calls to the billing department to report that she lived alone and had not made the numerous calls to Bordeaux that appeared on her bill. The billing department employees to whom she spoke had assured her each time that they would investigate and get back in touch with her, but she heard nothing until the disconnection threat arrived. When she contacted the billing department supervisor to express her dismay, the supervisor said, "Disconnection is not our responsibility." Mary Jo explained that it was unlikely she herself could convince the disconnection department not to continue her phone service while the billing department investigated the Bordeaux calls. She said, "I am in an impossible position, because for weeks your department personnel *have* told me it was their responsibility to deal with this, but they have not dealt with it. Now, as a result of their not carrying out what they said was their responsibility, I may lose my phone service, but you are telling me it is not up to you to help. Can you see my predicament? What would you do if you were in my position?" This story is one with a happy ending, because the supervisor realized that the technique was inappropriate, she wanted to help, and she did.

—Form self-help groups. Put up notices, place advertisements to try to find people in situations similar to yours, dealing with the same or similar experts or institutions. Most people find it easier to see that someone else has tried all they can than to see that they themselves have done so; therefore, it is strengthening to hear that other intelligent, sane people have been treated as badly as you. Self-help groups are also perfect for brainstorming, because two or twelve heads are better than one. Each of you may have tried techniques or routes that haven't occurred to the others, either because of your having access to different information and resources or because people with different personalities tend to think of different approaches. Dr. Marlene Levene studied women survivors of incest who discussed together their tendency to blame themselves for the harm that had been done to them when they were children.[10] For some, the self-blame had been fed by the perpetrators of the incest, and for others, mental health professionals had contributed to their self-blame by asking such questions as, "*Why* didn't you tell anyone as soon as it started happening to you?" The women reported that listening to one another's stories was a major factor in helping them to stop blaming themselves and get on with their lives, because as they saw that the *other* women had not been to blame, they began to understand that perhaps they themselves had not been at fault.

—Choose some action you can take that will go beyond meeting with others and providing moral support. Many people, knowing that activists are routinely branded as troublemakers, are reluctant to consider doing this and come to it only after lengthy, exhausting periods of mistreatment by a system. I urge you not to wait until your energy is so depleted that you feel you have no alternative *but* to take action. However, if you do wait until that point, you may discover that you are energized simply by talking to others about *planning* to do something for yourselves and to do it together. Some excellent books have been written about how to do such organizing and planning, and *Mother Jones* magazine's yearly list of "ordinary people" who have taken action and made a difference is a fine source of ideas and inspiration.

Put on paper your view of the problem that confronts you and, probably, them. For instance, Gray Panther founder Maggie Kuhn reports that, in starting action to organize older people to obtain their human rights, she sent out a statement of some problems she thought they shared. She says that she

> became more mad than sad. . . . I wrote a memo to five of my friends in the same fix: What are we going to do about it? We decided we would not abandon each other. We sent out working papers to all the retired people we could think of. We got an immediate response.[11]

But understand that you may have to spend a fair bit of time at the beginning simply stating what you see as the problem, bringing it up as often as possible to as many different people as possible. You may have to let it simmer in their minds until it "clicks" for them and then they contact you to say they are ready to join with you in some action. For instance, when eight-year-old Sam was in primary school, he suddenly started coming home looking pale and pinched. When his parents asked, he said nothing was wrong but that he didn't feel well. They took him to the pediatrician, who tested him for all sorts of physical problems. Luckily, Sam's mother happened to mention her worry about Sam to another parent whose child was in the same class. She said that her daughter had been coming home and "climbing the walls" after school, and the mother had been puzzled by this sudden change in her child. At that point, neither mother considered the possibility that something might be happening in the class. Instead, they assumed that their children were just at a difficult age and were handling it in their different styles. Then, however, a third mother mentioned that, while she was doing volunteer teacher-aide work in that classroom, she had observed that the teacher treated the students extremely harshly. Not infrequently, she yelled at them and humiliated them. At that point, the three mothers checked with other parents, found that their children had undergone sudden behavioral changes as well, and went as a group to see the principal. They learned that the teacher and her young child had been unexpectedly deserted by her husband and she was in a bad emotional state as a result. Owing to the parents' expressions of concern, the principal quickly arranged for this teacher to have a leave of absence.

Once you have found several people with a common problem, it is likely that each of you will feel more energized and hopeful about being able to get some response from the system in question. If you can meet together in person or communicate by letters or—more rapidly—by computer, have a brainstorming session about possible action you could plan. Make it a rule that, while brainstorming, no one is allowed to criticize or make mocking or pessimistic comments about whether any particular suggested action would be effective. Such a group can be amazingly creative and resourceful, often with great spirit and humor. Then, decide on a plan of action, including choosing a sequence of steps you can take if the first doesn't work and considering the risks and potential benefits of each step. A group of farmers who came together to fight for their rights

> had a tractorcade to Omaha, Nebraska, last September. That's about 130 miles. It took four days to get there. We tractorcaded from four different directions. There was some four hundred tractors when we all got there. My tractor and our bunch barricaded the main street downtown to keep the traffic out. We was kickin' off the Karkin-Gephardt bill to give us parity.

During the 130 miles, we got horns and waves supportin' us and some was givin' us the finger. Those was thirty-year-old people.[12]

In planning action, be aware that dealing with these systems and institutions can mean spending enormous amounts of time doing unpaid work. Don't be surprised if you feel angry about having to do such work because the system is unresponsive. It may help to think of it as volunteer work. Although volunteers in hospitals or charity organizations often do not receive the appreciation and respect that they deserve, at least they are not accused of being destructive for doing that work. Taking action aimed at holding systems and experts accountable and making them more humane can indeed be destructive to their irresponsible and inhumane features, but your aim is to help the powerless, as is the aim of volunteers who tutor children with learning problems or visit people who are too ill or disabled to leave their homes. The key difference, of course, is that volunteers who do their work but do not challenge the systems and experts are not accused of being troublemakers. Those who challenge the ways that systems and experts operate—even when the challenge is intended to assist those in need—are unfairly classified as bent on destruction.

If you find that you feel guilty because you are struggling to obtain humane treatment of yourself (rather than your parents, your partner, your children, your friends, or "the needy or oppressed" in general), *fight that feeling*! In the words of one organizer,

> "Don't mourn, organize!" said Joe Hill.... The institutional effects on the self we can try to fend off personally—fight for ourselves as hard as we'd fight for our children.[13]

If necessary, put a stop to the belief that you are "selfish" by realizing anything you accomplish is likely to help those who come after you, too.

—And again, whatever action you decide to take, remember to think of yourself as a daring pioneer.

DON'T

—Don't assume that the fault is yours, that your lack of understanding or success is a sign that you are stupid or inadequate.

—Don't assume that what the authorities say is absolutely, objectively true. Don't assume that they make only claims that are backed up by evidence. Each time I have ventured into a new field, whether a new institution or a new area of research, I have begun by assuming that the existing institution is a good one and the "established truths" in the research area represent reasonable thinking. Nearly every time, I have found that those assumptions have been unfounded. The amount of sloppiness and care-lessness in the treatment of people and the thinking about issues in most areas is absolutely astonishing.

So try the Giant Con Assumption: Assume that what you are being told may be far from true, and see whether that eases your search for the truth and for help.

—Don't assume that the authority is always right. If an expert says, "They have discovered that . . ." ask exactly who are "they." Be persistent until you get a reasonable response. Is this material published in a journal somewhere, backed up by research? If so, how can you obtain a copy of the article? I have taught full-year courses dealing with how badly most research is done and how many well-meaning people believe all sorts of untruths, just because they think researchers have proven them to be correct.[14]

—Don't idealize *any* expert. For reasons given here and in Chapters 4 through 7, that idealization is often unwarranted. And if you are too busily idealizing the speaker or writer, you will find it harder to evaluate thoroughly the merits of their words. In any case, the experts who have the least to hide tend to be the least likely to encourage you to believe they are infallible.

—Don't settle for doublespeak and other jargon from the authorities and experts, and don't get caught up in using it yourself. If one of them tells you, then, that your child has "minimal brain dysfunction," immediately ask them to explain in precise, simple terms what that means and what the evidence is. And absolutely *never* use the jargon yourself. There is no excuse for jargon and complexity. Even some medical people are beginning to write papers making the point that fancy, technical-sounding medical conditions can be explained in plain English to just about anyone. So ask persistently for clear, simple explanations. When I advise my Ph.D. students about how to write their doctoral dissertations or papers for a scholarly audience, I suggest that they write so that a twelve-year-old could understand.

Why should we think that physicians, for instance, can understand things *we* cannot possibly comprehend? Remember that doctors used to be the kids next door, and some of them graduated at the bottom of their medical school class. When I have accompanied doctors on hospital rounds, the only times I have seen a patient unable to understand what a doctor said was when the doctor wasn't trying to be clear.

—Don't assume that the authorities' or experts' top priority is serving those whom they are supposed to help. Don't assume, then, that all doctors care first and foremost about healing, that all lawyers care most about seeing justice done for their clients, that educators care most about teaching, and so on. In a prominent U.S. law school, a law student was accused of having cheated on an examination. Members of the law school administration questioned some of the people seated near him during the exam, but the accused was not allowed to question them *or* to defend himself by speaking. He was simply dismissed from the school, a significant irony, because the opportunity to cross-examine witnesses and to choose to testify in one's own behalf are essential principles of our legal system.

I hope that some of these strategies will fortify you as you try to get what you need from authorities and experts. It will be a fine beginning if they help you stop feeling stupid and powerless, if you become less inclined to blame yourself for the inhumanity, inefficiency, and inadequacy of the system.

9

Taking Heart

Why should we be well-adjusted to a maladjusted situation?
Silence means consent. We must put a stop to passive obedi-
ence, self-effacing dedication, and loyalty to institutions.
—Laura Gasparis Vonfrolio, founder of the magazine *Revolution: The Journal of Nurse Empowerment*[1]

As individuals, we feel happier, clearer in our thinking, and less
ashamed of ourselves when we can see clearly that the obstacles in our way when we seek help are often not of our own
making. If you find some parts of this book useful, I hope you
won't believe that things are better now because you changed
what was wrong with you. If I have been helpful, it is not
because you needed fixing. It was because systems don't spon-
taneously show us how they work and where their faults lie.
Sometimes we need encouragement to focus on those factors
and stop berating ourselves. And I hope you will have more
confidence in your own view of what is happening to you, for

as Jean Alonso has written, she asked a woman named Ellie, "How did you get out of your feelings of depression?" and Ellie replied, "I got back in touch with my own priorities, my own sense of myself."[2]

As a society, we would be healthier and stronger—and some institutions would be less monolithic and tyrannical—if both service providers and those who seek their services could openly acknowledge each other's strengths and limitations. We shall be able to change these disempowering systems only when enough of us see that the problem is not us, when we call their bluff and insist on change. The change can be as specific as consumers' recently effective demand for truthful labeling on foods or as general as more humane attitudes toward clients by professionals.

Would that we all had the drive and energy that Gray Panther founder and prime mover Maggie Kuhn has put into working for change. Studs Terkel interviewed her when she was eighty-two:

> Though she appears frail, her manner, her voice, are vibrant. Her energy is astonishing; as is her schedule. "I am going to Hopkinsville, Kentucky, this afternoon. Then I'm flying to Toledo to try to raise some money. Then I fly to San Francisco to do an all-day program at the University of California."[3]

And it was Kuhn who said, "I wish that people would not always put themselves down, fearing their own lack of power. The empowerment of the powerless is a beautiful thing."[4]

Notes

Chapter 1 You're Smarter Than They Make You Feel

1. Caplan and Wilson, 1990. Also relevant to this topic is the following excerpt from a 1992 report, about a psychologist's report in a child custody proceeding, from the Ontario Board of Examiners in Psychology:

   "[In the psychologist's report,] recommendations and conclusions were based on facts for which the reliability and/or validity had not been sufficiently established; . . . based on an inadequate investigation and assessment of significant facts and issues; . . . in the absence of sufficient psychological data or evidence and were not based on any accepted psychological theory. . . .

   He submitted a report effectively recommending a change in custody and access arrangements to a child without,

   (a) interviewing and/or assessing significant individuals, including:

   (i)   the child's mother and custodial parent;

   (ii) the child's sister;

   (iii) the woman currently cohabiting with the child's father. . . .

   He submitted a report . . . without obtaining corroboration or confirmation of the information provided to him.

   [The psychologist] strongly recommended that the child be allowed to accompany her father out of the country.

181

. . . [The psychologist's] statements . . . about the mother's environment, e.g., 'it would appear that her mother's environment was oppressive, restrictive, emotionally volatile and essentially unsatisfying' were based on the observation of a twelve year old made during a single session." pp. 11–12

2. Caplan, 1987.
3. Steinem, 1992, p. 119.
4. Angelou, 1970, pp. 151–152.
5. Masson, 1990.
6. Middlebrook, 1992, and Millett, 1990.
7. Sacks, 1982.
8. Byatt, 1992, p. 86.
9. Caplan, 1988.
10. Caplan, 1989.
11. Terkel, 1988.
12. Terkel, 1988, pp. 86–87.
13. Sanford & Donovan, 1984.
14. White, 1980.
15. Caplan, 1989.
16. For example, Henley, 1977.

Chapter 2 What They Say and What They Don't Say

1. Steinem, 1992.
2. Pirsig, 1991, p. 118.
3. Caplan, 1993b.
4. Terkel, 1988, p. 101.
5. Johnston, 1990, p. 3.
6. Kramer, 1984, p. 58.
7. Pilisuk, 1990, pp. 16–17.
8. MacPherson, G., 1990.
9. Terkel, 1988, p. 345.
10. Gottschall, 1986.
11. *Globe and Mail*, 1990, p. A1; see also Gordon, 1990.
12. *Random House Dictionary*, 1967.
13. Rounds, 1993, p. 35.
14. Carniol, 1990, p. 59.

15. Johnston, 1990, pp. 3–4.
16. Terkel, 1988, pp. 99–100.

Chapter 3 What They Do and What They Don't Do

1. Kramer, 1984, p. 111.
2. Johnston, 1990, p. 2.
3. Bell, 1992, who cites Bennet, 1991.
4. Henderson, 1990, p. 59.
5. Ibid., p. 60.
6. Steinem, 1992.
7. Terkel, 1988, p. 342.
8. Ibid.
9. Terkel, 1988, p. 344.
10. Kramer, 1984, pp. 61–62.

Chapter 4 Why Do They Act That Way?

1. Atwood, 1991, p. 7.
2. McIntosh, 1985.
3. Carniol, 1990, p. 67.
4. Caplan, 1989.
5. Pilisuk, 1990, p. 118.
6. Peach, 1975; Brody, 1980; cited by Gans, 1991.
7. Henley, 1977.
8. Atwood, 1991, p. 64.
9. Landers, 1992b, p. J4.
10. Kramer, 1984, p. 45.
11. Friend, 1990, p. 1A.
12. Pilisuk, 1990, p. 18.
13. Nazario, 1992, p. B6.
14. Carniol, 1990, p. 62.
15. Friedson, 1970, cited by Gans, 1991.
16. Henley, 1977; Leary, 1957; Miller, 1986.
17. Henley, 1977.
18. Carniol, 1990, p. 50.
19. Caplan, 1985.
20. Gans, 1991; Burgess, 1989, cited by Gans.
21. Carniol, 1990, p. 57.

22. Rounds, 1993, p. 37.
23. Pizzo, Fricker, & Hogan, 1993, p. 18.
24. Steinem, 1992, pp. 189–90.

Chapter 5 Asking Questions: Why It's Done So Rarely

1. Masson, 1993, p. 174.
2. Caplan, Secord-Gilbert, and Staton, 1990.
3. Caplan & Caplan, 1994.
4. Atwood, 1991, p. 61.
5. Caplan, 1989.
6. Ibid.
7. AIDS overlooked, 1993.
8. Hamilton, 1992.
9. Ibid., p. 96.
10. Birns, 1985.
11. Chess & Thomas, 1982.
12. Rush, 1980; Masson, 1984.
13. MacQueen, 1992, p. A25.
14. Ibid.
15. Landers, 1992a, p. H4.
16. Orenstein, 1993, p. 56.
17. United States Commission on Civil Rights, 1973.
18. Kinsbourne, 1978.
19. Wine, 1985.
20. Kohlberg, 1976; Kohlberg & Kramer, 1969.
21. Gilligan, 1982.
22. Kramer, 1984, p. 109.
23. Ubelacker, 1993, p. B2.
24. Gordon, 1990, p. 360.
25. Henderson, 1990, p. 59.
26. Henderson, 1990, p. 60.

Chapter 6 What Limits Experts' Critical Thinking?

1. Carniol, 1990, p. 67.
2. Atwood, 1991, p. 4.
3. Grant, 1992.

4. Solinger, 1993, p. 19.
5. Nielsen et al., 1970.
6. Caplan, 1989.
7. Cromie, 1993, p. 5.
8. Palter & D'Argo, 1993.
9. Ibid.; Butler, 1992.
10. Palter & D'Argo, 1993; Butler, 1992.
11. Palter & d'Argo, 1993.
12. Dye & Roth, 1990.
13. Ibid., p. 119.
14. Caplan, 1987.
15. Ubelacker, 1993, p. B2.
16. Rounds, 1993.
17. DiManno, 1993, p. A7.
18. MacPherson, J., 1993.
19. Kramer, 1984, p. 205.
20. Pirsig, 1991, p. 58.
21. Hudson, 1972.
22. Caplan, 1993a.
23. Pirsig, 1991, p. 58.
24. Caplan, 1993a.
25. Hamilton, 1992, pp. 96–97.
26. Ibid., p. 97.
27. Rounds, 1993, p. 35.
28. Moore, 1990.
29. Kramer, 1984, p. 189.
30. Friday, 1977.
31. Erikson, 1968.
32. Caplan, 1979.
33. Sylvester, 1992, p. 27.
34. France, 1993, p. 9.
35. My italics, Ibid.
36. Atwood, 1991, p. 6.
37. Seiden, 1992.
38. Ibid., p. B1.
39. Kramer, 1984, pp. 130–31.
40. Levy, 1993, p. K14.

Chapter 7 What Limits Consumers' Critical Thinking

1. Atwood, 1991.
2. Kramer, 1984, p. 48.
3. Kramer, 1984, p. 189.
4. Wolfe, 1991, p. D1.
5. Ibid.
6. Johnston, 1990; Illich, 1975.
7. Atwood, 1991, p. 5.
8. Hamilton, 1992, pp. 92–93.
9. Sacks, 1982, p. 171.
10. Caplan and Gans, 1991, p. A17.
11. Davidson, 1991.
12. Ibid.
13. Ibid., p. 13.
14. Ibid., p. 14.
15. Maynard, 1992, p. 12.
16. Laframboise, 1993, p. A17.
17. Atwood, 1991, pp. 64–65.

Chapter 8 Reacting and Resisting, Saving Your Sanity

1. Gerrard, 1990.
2. Huck & Sandler, 1979.
3. Kirwin, 1970.
4. Sacks, 1982, p. 105.
5. Ibid., pp. 109 and 158.
6. Storch, 1990.
7. Atwood, 1991, pp. 63–64.
8. Ibid., p. 88.
9. Pilisuk, 1990, p. 18.
10. Levene, 1992.
11. Terkel, 1988, p. 343.
12. Terkel, 1988, p. 104.
13. Alonso, 1991, p. 13.
14. Caplan & Caplan, 1994.

Chapter 9 Taking Heart

1. Rounds, 1993, p. 38.
2. Alonso, 1991, p. 13.
3. Terkel, 1988, p. 342.
4. Ibid.

Bibliography

This is by no means a comprehensive list of the many fine works whose authors have written thoughtfully and questioningly about various institutions. It is limited for the most part to references I have cited in the text.

AIDS overlooked in seniors, MDs say. (1993). *Toronto Star*, Jan. 12, 1993, p. C1.

Alonso, Jean. (1991). In the belly of the beast. *The Women's Review of Books VIII*, nos. 10–11 (July): 12–13.

Angelou, Maya. (1970). *I know why the caged bird sings*. New York: Bantam.

Atwood, Glenna Wotton. (1991). *Living well with Parkinson's*. New York: Wiley.

Begley, Sharon. (1993). The meaning of junk: What's "good" science? The Supreme Court tackles the question. *Newsweek*, March 22, pp. 62–64.

Bell, Derrick. (1992). *Faces at the bottom of the well: The permanence of racism*. New York: BasicBooks.

Bennet, James. (1991). Thieving lawyers draining client security funds, *New York Times*, Dec. 27, p. B16.

Bevan, W. (1976). The sound of the wind that's blowing. *American Psychologist 5*, 115–24.

Birns, Beverly. (1985). The mother-infant tie: Fifty years of theory, science and science fiction. Work in Progress No. 21, Stone Center for Developmental Services and Studies. Wellesley, Mass.: Wellesley College.

Brody, D. S. (1980). The patient's role in clinical decision-making. *Annals of Internal Medicine 93*, 718–22.

Brook, R. H. (1973). Effectiveness of non-emergency care via an emergency room. *Annals of Internal Medicine 78*, 333–39.

Burgess, M. M. (1989). Ethical and economic aspects of non-compliance and overtreatment. *Canadian Medical Association Journal 141*, 777–80.

Butler, Sandra. (1992). Personal communication.

Byatt, A. S. (1992). *The virgin in the garden*. New York: Vintage International.

Caplan, Paula J. (1993a). *Lifting a ton of feathers: A woman's guide to surviving in an academic world*. Toronto: University of Toronto Press.

Caplan, Paula J. (1993b). *The myth of women's masochism* (Revised edition). Toronto: University of Toronto Press.

Caplan, Paula J. (1989). *Don't blame mother: Mending the mother-daughter relationship*. New York: Harper and Row.

Caplan, Paula J. (1988). Confusing terms and false dichotomies: A plea for logical thinking about learning disabilities. *Orbit*, 14–15.

Caplan, Paula J. (1987). *The myth of women's masochism*. New York: Signet. (paperback with additional chapter)

Caplan, Paula J. (1979). Erikson's concept of inner space: A data-based re-evaluation. *American Journal of Orthopsychiatry 49*, 100–108.

Caplan, Paula J., & Caplan, Jeremy B. (1994). *Thinking critically about research on sex and gender*. New York: HarperCollins.

Caplan, Paula J., & Gans, Maureen. (1991). Does scientific expertise equal truth? *Toronto Star*, Mar. 25, p. A17.

Caplan, Paula J.; Secord-Gilbert, Margaret; & Staton, Pat. (1990). *Teaching children to think critically about sexism and other forms of bias*. Toronto: Green Dragon Press.

Caplan, Paula J., & Wilson, Jeffery. (1990). Assessing the child custody assessors. *Reports of Family Law*, Oct. 25, pp. 121–34.

Carniol, Ben. (1990). *Case critical: Challenging social work in Canada*, 2d ed. Toronto: Between the Lines.

Chess, Stella, & Thomas, Alexander. (1982). Infant bonding: Mystique and reality. *American Journal of Orthopsychiatry 52*, 213–22.

Conway, J. (1988). Differences among clinical psychologists: Scientists, practitioners, and scientist-practitioners. *Professional Psychology: Research and Practice 6*, 642–55.

Coons, W. H. (1990). The crooked path. *Canadian Psychology/ Psychologie canadienne 31*, 138–46.

Cromie, William J. (1993). Father's role in birth defects probed. *Radcliffe News*, Winter, pp. 5–6.

Dale, Jennifer, & Foster, Peggy. (1986). *Feminists and state welfare*. London: Routledge & Kegan Paul.

Davidson, Keay. (1991). Nature vs. nurture. *San Francisco Examiner*, Jan. 20, pp. 10–17.

DiManno, Rosie. (1993). Internal police tribunals still unfair to women. *Toronto Star*, Jan. 15, p. A7.

Dye, Ellen, & Roth, Susan. (1990). Psychotherapists' knowledge about and attitudes toward sexual assault victim clients. *Psychology of Women Quarterly 14*, 191–212.

Erikson, Erik. (1968). *Identity, youth, and crisis*. New York: Norton.

Erikson, Erik. (1951). Sex differences in the play configurations of preadolescents. *American Journal of Orthopsychiatry 21*, 667–92.

France, Antoinette. (1993). Blowing the whistle: The costs and consequences of speaking out in the workplace. *Radcliffe News*, Winter, p. 9.

Freeman, Gordon. (1990). Kinetics of nonhomogenous processes in human society: Unethical behavior and societal chaos. *Canadian Journal of Physics 68*, 794–98.

Friday, Nancy. (1977) *My Mother/MySelf*. New York: Delacorte.

Friedson, E. (1970). *Profession of medicine*. New York: Dodd, Mead.

Friend, Tim. (1990). Perks affect how doctors choose drugs. *USA Today*, Dec. 12, p. A1.

Gans, Maureen. (1991). *Mother bears on the rampage: The politics of caring for chronically ill children*. Unpublished paper, Ontario Institute for Studies in Education. Toronto.

Gerrard, Nikki. (1990). Racism and sexism, together, in mental health systems: The voices of women of color. Doctoral dissertation, University of Toronto.

Gilligan, Carol. (1982). *In a different voice.* Cambridge, Mass.: Harvard University Press.

Globe and Mail. (1990). Study gives new explanation of awful truth about weight, May 24, p. A1.

Gordon, James S. (1990). Holistic medicine and mental health practice: A new synthesis. *American Journal of Orthopsychiatry 60,* 357–70.

Gottschall, Elaine. (1986). *Food and the gut reaction: Intestinal health through diet for Crohn's disease, ulcerative colitis, diverticulitis, celiac disease, cystic fibrosis, chronic diarrhea.* Kirkton, Ont.: Kirkton Press.

Grant, Nicole J. (1992). *The selling of contraception: The Dalkon Shield case, sexuality, and women's autonomy.* Athens: Ohio State University Press.

Greer, Germaine. (1992). *The change: Women, aging and the menopause.* New York: Knopf.

Hamilton, Jean A. (1992). Biases in women's health research. *Women and Therapy 12,* 91–101.

Henderson, Jim. (1990). When scientists fake it. *American Way,* Mar. 1, pp. 56–62, 100–101.

Henley, Nancy. (1977). *Body politics: Power, sex, and nonverbal communication.* Englewood Cliffs, N.J.: Prentice-Hall.

Hogan, R. (1979). An interview with Robert Hogan. *APA Monitor 20,* no. 4, 4–5.

Horgan, Paul. (1966). *Things as they Are.* New York: Noonday Press.

Huck, Schuyler W., & Sandler, Howard M. (1979). *Rival hypotheses: Alternative interpretations of data-based conclusions.* New York: Harper and Row.

Hudson, Liam. (1972). *The cult of the fact.* London: Cape.

Illich, Ivan. (1975). *Medical nemesis: The expropriation of health.* London: Calder & Boyars.

Johnston, Corinne. (1990). Beyond dependence: A feminist perspective to empowerment in the health care system. Paper presented at Wilfrid Laurier University and Ontario Institute for Studies in Education Conference on Community Psychology. Waterloo, Ont. Apr. 20.

Kinsbourne, Marcel. (1978). Personal communication.

Kirwin, Paul. (1970). Affect expression training in psychiatric patients: The verbalization of feeling-cause relationships. Durham, N.C.: Veterans Administration Hospital. Unpublished manuscript.

Kohl, Herbert. (1992). *From archetype to zeitgeist: Powerful ideas for powerful thinking*. Boston: Little, Brown.

Kohlberg, Lawrence. (1976). Moral stages and moralization: The cognitive-developmental approach. In T. Lickona (ed.), *Moral development and behavior: Theory, research, and social issues*. New York: Holt, Rinehart, and Winston.

Kohlberg, Lawrence, & Kramer, Richard. (1969). Continuities and discontinuities in child and adult moral development. *Human Development 12*, 93–120.

Kramer, Mark. (1984). *Invasive procedures: A year in the world of two surgeons*. New York: Penguin.

Laframboise, Donna. (1993). Patients take charge of their own care. *Toronto Star*, Apr. 5, p. A17.

Landers, Ann. (1992a). *Toronto Star*, Aug. 8, p. H4.

Landers, Ann. (1992b). *Toronto Star*, Oct. 17, p. J4.

Leary, Timothy. (1957). *Interpersonal diagnosis of personality*. New York: Ronald Press.

Levene, Marlene. (1992). Women's experience of self-blame for incestuous abuse: A feminist analysis. Doctoral dissertation, University of Toronto.

Levy, Harold. (1993). Comedy and tragedy in court. *Toronto Star*, Mar. 27, p. K14.

MacPherson, Gael. (1990). The construct of auditory processing: Validation and assessment. Doctoral dissertation, University of Toronto.

MacPherson, J. (1993). Letter on behalf of Survivors of Medical Abuse, to Health Professions Regulatory Advisory Council. Toronto, January 18.

MacQueen, Ken. (1992). Academia goes for the judicial jugular. *Toronto Star*, Dec. 18, p. A25.

Masson, Jeffrey Moussaieff. (1993). *My father's guru: A journey through spirituality and disillusion*. Reading, MA: Addison-Wesley.

Masson, Jeffrey Moussaieff. (1990). *Final analysis: The making and unmaking of a psychoanalyst*. Reading, Mass. Addison Wesley.

Masson, Jeffrey Moussaieff. (1984). *The assault on truth: Freud's suppression of the seduction theory*. New York: Farrar, Straus, & Giroux.

Maynard, Joyce. (1992). Charting my own course. *Newsweek*, Dec. 21, p. 12.

McIntosh, Peggy. (1985). Feeling like a fraud. Work-in-Progress Series, No. 18. Wellesley, Mass.: Stone Center, Wellesley College.

Mendelsohn, Robert S. (1982). *Male practice*. Chicago: Contemporary Books.

Middlebrook, Diane Wood. (1992). *Anne Sexton: A biography*. New York: Vintage.

Miller, Jean Baker. (1986). *Toward a new psychology of women*, 2d ed. Boston: Beacon Press.

Millett, Kate. (1990). *The loony-bin trip*. New York: Simon and Schuster.

Moore, Patricia. (1990). Personal communication.

Nazario, Sonia L. (1992). Medical science seeks a cure for doctors suffering from boorish bedside manner. *Wall Street Journal*, Mar. 17, pp. B1, B6.

Nielsen, J., et al. (1970). Klinefelter's syndrome in children. *Journal of Child Psychology and Psychiatry 11*, 109–19.

Office of Technology Assessment (Congressional, U.S.). (1978). *Assessing the safety and efficacy of medical technology*. Washington, D.C.: Author.

Ontario Board of Examiners in Psychology. (1992). *The bulletin*. Volume 19, Number 2, pp. 11–16.

Orenstein, Peggy. (1993). Schooling girls. *Mother Jones* Jan./Feb., p. 56.

Palter, Jay, & D'Argo, Joan. (1993). Cancer establishment studiously avoids pollution link. *The Toronto Star*, January 11, p. A15.

Peach, M.L. (1975). Freire's process of conscientization and an analysis of a community health care attitude survey. Master's thesis, University of Toronto.

Pilisuk, Marc. (1990). Unaffordable denial [A review of Chellis Glendinning (1990). *When technology wounds: The human consequences of progress.* NY: William Morrow.] *READINGS: A Journal of Reviews and Commentary in Mental Health.* December, pp. 16–19.

Pirsig, Robert M. (1991). *Lila.* New York: Bantam.

Pizzo, Stephen, with Mary Fricker and Kevin Hogan. (1993). Shredded justice. *Mother Jones,* Jan./Feb/, 17–23.

Random House Dictionary. (1967). Stein, Jess (ed.). New York: Random House.

Robbins, Tom. (1990). *Skinny legs and all.* New York: Bantam.

Robertson, P. J. M. (1990). Comfort and strategy for a life in literature. [Review of Joseph Gold. *Read for your life: Literature as a life support system.* Toronto: Fitzhenry and Whiteside.] *Toronto Star,* June 2, p. C21.

Rounds, Kate. (1993). Report from the ward. *Ms.* Jan.-Feb., pp. 33–39.

Rush, Florence. (1980). *The best kept secret: Sexual abuse of children.* New York: Prentice-Hall.

Sacks, Oliver. (1982). *A leg to stand on.* New York: Harper-Collins.

Sanford, Linda Tschirhart, & Donovan, Mary Ellen. (1984). *Women and self-esteem: Understanding and improving the way we think and feel about ourselves.* New York: Penguin.

Seiden, Howard. (1992). What to demand when having a mammogram. *Toronto Star,* Dec. 17, p. B1.

Sjoo, Monica, & Mor, Barbara. (1987). *The great cosmic mother: Rediscovering the religion of the earth.* San Francisco: Harper and Row.

Solinger, Rickie. (1993). A cautionary tale (Review of Nicole J. Grant's book, *The selling of contraception: The Dalkon Shield case, sexuality, and women's autonomy*). *The Women's Review of Books X* (Jan.): 19.

Steinem, Gloria. (1992). *Revolution from within: A book of self-esteem.* Boston: Little, Brown.

Storch, Debby. (1990). Personal communication.

Sylvester, Martin. (1992). Review of T. Byram Karasu, *Wisdom in the practice of psychotherapy. READINGS: A Journal of Reviews and Commentary in Mental Health,* Dec. p. 27.

Tavris, Carol. (1992). *The mismeasure of woman: Why women are not the better sex, the inferior sex, or the opposite sex.* New York: Simon and Schuster.

Terkel, Studs. (1988). *The great divide: Second thoughts on the American dream.* New York: Pantheon.

Thorngate, Warren. (1990). The economy of attention and the development of psychology. *Canadian Psychology/Psychologie canadienne 31,* 262–73.

Tulving, E., & Madigan, S. A. (1970). Memory and verbal learning. *Annual Review of Psychology 21.* Palo Alto, Calif.: Annual Reviews.

Ubelacker, Sheryl. (1993). Doctors' 'god' status questioned by boomers. *Toronto Star,* Jan. 11, p. B2.

United States Commission on Civil Rights. (1973). *Teachers and students: Differences in teacher interaction with Mexican-American and Anglo Students.* Washington, D.C.: U.S. Government Printing Office.

White, Georgina. (1980). Attributions about women: A foundation for barriers. *Resources for Feminist Research/Documentation sur la recherche feministe 9,* 9.

Williams, R. (1977). *The wonderful world within you.* New York: Bantam.

Wine, Jeri Dawn. (1985). Toward a feminist standpoint for psychology. *Popular Feminism Papers, No. 2.* Toronto: Centre for Women's Studies in Education, Ontario Institute for Studies in Education.

Wolfe, Morris. (1991). Cross current: Why does a scholarly journal publish prejudice passed off as science? *Globe and Mail,* July 18, p. D1.

Women pay more, get less, report finds. (1993). *Springfield (Missouri) News-Leader,* May 18, p. 1A.

Wong, Tony. (1990). Panel finds 1 in 7 MDs are badly deficient. *Toronto Star*, Dec. 17, p. A3.

Zola, I. K. (1978). Medicine as an institution of social control. In J. Ehrenreich (ed.), *The cultural crisis of modern medicine*. New York: Monthly Review Press, pp. 80–100.

Index